CHRISTIAN WITNESS
IN A
POSTMODERN
WORLD

CHRISTIAN WITNESS
IN A
POSTMODERN
WORLD

HARRY LEE POE

ABINGDON PRESS / NASHVILLE

CHRISTIAN WITNESS IN A POSTMODERN WORLD

Copyright © 2001 by Harry Lee Poe

Library of Congress Cataloging-in-Publication Data

Poe, Harry Lee, 1950–
    Christian witness in a postmodern world / Harry Lee Poe.
        p.   cm.
    Includes index.
ISBN 0-687-04931-8 (alk. paper)
    1. Evangelistic work—United States.   I. Title.

BV3790 .P565 2001
269'.2—dc21   00-067379

01 02 03 04 05 06 07 08 09 10—10 9 8 7 6 5 4 3 2 1

MANUFACTURED IN THE UNITED STATES OF AMERICA

TO

CHAPLAIN JAMES H. DENT

MENTOR, COLLEAGUE, FRIEND

CONTENTS

PREFACE

In the late 1970s I read all the novels of Walker Percy, through whom I first learned the expression "postmodernism." Throughout the late-1960s and 1970s I had monitored the cultural changes taking place in my world, but Percy was the first one to give the changes a label. Not until the early 1990s, however, did I hear anyone within the theological community paying attention to this phenomenon.

Most of what people write about postmodernism seems to fall within two basic groups. Either they think postmodernism is "the best thing since sliced bread" and everyone should throw care to the wind, or they think that postmodernism needs to be beaten down with a stick never to rise again. I think this book takes a third approach, which recognizes how postmodernism could arise, recognizes its dangers, but also recognizes opportunities it creates for the advance of the gospel. This book does not argue that we should abandon rationality and truth, on the other hand it recognizes that we can never go back to the prevailing cultural norms of the past.

Some people see their task as destroying old cultural forms while others see their task as preserving the tradition at all costs. I am concerned that people who are different from me have a clear and simple opportunity to meet Jesus Christ through the gospel. It is not necessary that they become rationalists in order to have faith. At least, our experience in the modern mission movement suggests this and the Bible seems to place no such barrier to faith. Evangelism has been so easy for so long in the West that we have gotten lazy about it. The advent of postmodern thinking will force Christians to erase all the cultural assumptions from their practice of religion and recapture the vitality of simple New Testament faith, which arose in a pluralistic culture.

In many ways, we have returned to a first-century context in the West in which the church has no special status. The new custodians of the popular culture may be hostile to the Christian faith, but the general population no longer knows much about it. As Bishop Lesslie Newbigin has suggested, the United States now constitutes a mission field as though the gospel had never been preached here before. The old assumptions of Christendom no longer hold. The church has lost North America and Europe as she once lost North Africa and the Middle East. The question to be answered is whether or not she will regain these lands.

Postmodernity looms for many as the great challenge, as though post-modernity will cause us to lose the West. The church lost the West a generation ago. The culture wars are long over. If anything, postmodernity represents a rattling of the old modern biases against Christ contained in modern Western culture. With each dreadful aspect of postmodernity, which frightens all true modernists to the bone, we will see the possibility of a bridge or doorway for the gospel. Postmodernity, while leaving the assump-tions of the West far behind, may actually provide the context for the re-evangelization of the West. To succeed, we must travel to a different place and culture: our own home as it moves into the future. As we move into this new world, we can do so with the comfort of knowing that Christians have faced this same challenge over and over for two thousand years.

I first stepped out of my culture when, at the age of sixteen, I moved to Washington to serve as a page in the United States Senate. I lived on my own in a boarding house a few blocks from the Capitol. While there I gained an education in cultural values. In the past, race relations had always been a black and white issue! In Washington, however, I learned about a vast array of people I should hate. People quizzed me on why I was friends with the Puerto Rican, the Jew, the Pole, and the Italian. Years would pass before I took a course in cultural anthropology, which first stirred my interest in understanding culture. I continue to owe a debt to Bryant Hicks, who taught that course and later became my colleague when I joined the faculty of Southern Baptist Theological Seminary. Another experience in seminary that sealed my interest in the issue of culture came when Willis Bennett took ten students to New York City for a week in July. On a hot sidewalk he bought me my first frozen yogurt. He exposed me to a world of other experiences that week that had a profound effect on my thinking. We stood on another street corner and he said to me, "Twenty thousand people live on this block." At the front of each building stood a doorman to restrict entrance. Old-fashioned visitation would not work here. I began to ask a question I continue to ask: How can they hear the gospel?

During my doctoral studies, my major professor, Lewis A. Drummond, encouraged me to spend part of a year at Oxford University to gain a broader intellectual foundation. There I made friends with people from all over the world who were the heirs of the British Empire. The experience put American ways of doing things in perspective.

When I finished seminary, I served four years as a prison chaplain in the medium-security Kentucky State Reformatory near Louisville while I pursued my doctoral studies. In the prison I learned what it meant to cross cultural boundaries and minister to people of different cultures. I first learned to relate to people who had entirely different belief systems. I am indebted to the principal chaplain, James H. Dent, and to our colleagues Darrell Rollins and Larry Vance for helping me understand prison culture. Chaplain Rollins also helped me understand black culture. My first book, *The Fruit of Christ's Presence,* came out of a Bible study I led with Chaplain Rollins, which I later developed into a sermon series as pastor of Simpsonville Baptist Church. My second book, *The Gospel and Its Meaning,* crystallized for me when Chaplain Rollins was asked to lead a chaplains retreat after I had become a seminary professor of evangelism. This book came about as the result of an invitation by Chaplain Dent to lead another chaplains retreat.

The bulk of this material formed the basis of the retreat. I am indebted to the chaplains who participated in the retreat sponsored by the generous support of Prison Fellowship of Kentucky under the leadership of Rick Drewitz. Contributing to the conversation that helped me refine the material were Fred Coburn, Larry Franklin, Bishop Carter, John Lentz, Suzanne McElwain, Tim O'Dell, John Ramsey, Peter Houck, Jim Dent, and Darrell Rollins.

The material further developed when I was asked to lead a seminar on "Apologetics in a Postmodern World" for the C. S. Lewis Institute in Oxford and Cambridge in the summer of 1998. I deeply appreciate Stan Mattson, president of the C. S. Lewis Foundation, and Karen Mulder, director of the arts track for the Institute, for their invitation to participate and their encouragement to develop this material as a book. Those who took part in the seminar further helped to clarify my thought. While they do not necessarily agree with my analysis, conclusions, or strategy, I appreciate their willingness to take part in the discussion. I particularly want to thank those who made presentations in the seminar: James I. Packer, Peter Kreeft, Dallas Willard, Bill Dembski, and Kelly Monroe. I owe MariAnne Van Eerden my deepest thanks for her tireless efforts in arranging the logistics that allowed such a notable collection of participants in the seminar.

My colleagues in the Academy for Evangelism in Theological Education have always provided a sounding board for ideas and a rich source of insight. Ron Johnson, professor of evangelism at the McAfee School of Theology of Mercer University, has been in a conversation with me about these issues for fifteen years. We hope we have stimulated one another's thought a little. *The Journal of the Academy for Evangelism in Theological Education* also published the germ of this book as an article entitled "Making the Most of Postmodernity."

I could not have completed this work without the support of those closest to me. Great portions of the manuscript were carefully and patiently put together by the tireless efforts of my secretary, Suzanne Nadaskay. The president, David Dockery, has allowed me both the time and the resources necessary to participate in the conferences, retreats, and annual meetings that made this book possible. My colleague Jimmy Davis with whom I have collaborated on other books related to science and religion is always helpful in thinking through any issue and asking the right question to make me think things further. I have also relied for many years on the insight and knowledge of L. Joseph Rosas III with whom I sat in philosophy seminars more than twenty years ago, and with whom I have discussed issues of post-modernity innumerable times since.

My wife, Mary Anne Poe, has been my greatest encouragement and friend in ministry. She has served on the pastoral staffs of several churches and now directs the social work program at Union University. I could not begin to credit all of her help, though she compelled me to accept the invitation to participate in the C. S. Lewis Institute when it would mean being away from the family for two weeks in the summer. Her most recent contribution came this morning when she asked, "Didn't you mean to say something about the 'whiteness' of the counterculture?" I did, but I forgot.

Harry Lee Poe
Jackson, Tennessee
June 3, 2000

INTRODUCTION

In 1967 Sidney Poitier and Rod Steiger starred in a dramatic blockbuster that focused attention on racial hatred and the possibility of finding common ground. *In the Heat of the Night* told the story of how a white rural southern sheriff and a black northern urban detective moved beyond their mutual prejudice and suspicion to develop a basis for working together. In the climax of the movie a lynch mob prepared to hang the black man, but in a moment they turned from their hostility. The entire plot of the movie hinged on the white and black races being united in their view of right and wrong. Every identifiable group has its own spin on what it likes and what is does not like, which usually gets translated into what is right and wrong. What a group likes are its prejudices; but what is right is the truth, whether the group likes it or not.

The mob suspected the black man of raping a white woman. The mob did not like this kind of behavior. The mob probably would not have approved of a white man raping a white woman, but it took the black man to turn the group into a mob. If a white man had been suspected, then they would have thought that the woman probably deserved it, and a mob would not have emerged. Such is the reasoning of "the group." For *In the Heat of the Night* to work, the white mob had to be so shocked and appalled by a white man's behavior that they would turn away from their black victim. The movie had to draw on a crime so deep-seated in the common understanding of both black and white people that its exposure would stop a mob. It had to be something of greater emotional intensity than racial hatred, because its recognition would leave no place for racial hatred. Such is the power of truth over preference.

In the movie *In the Heat of the Night,* the black and white communities find common ground in their shared horror of abortion. Thirty years later this powerful story of racial struggle would no longer work. It depends on a universally shared view of abortion that no longer exists. For the story to work, the audience must cringe at the notion of abortion. The audience cringed in 1967, but today the average viewer would be left asking, "What's the big deal?" What has happened in thirty years to the sense of right and wrong, which people possessed even when they did not like what happened or what it caused them to do. The mob did not like the idea of letting the black man go. Without an overriding sense of right and wrong, people are free to follow their prejudices, which become self-authenticating in a relativistic society.

Well-meaning people debate whether or not the United States was ever a Christian nation. The debate is rather academic, however, compared with the reality that Christians face at the close of the twentieth century. When I was a prison chaplain, the men on the yard had a great deal to say about "prison religion," which appeared shortly before a man was scheduled to go before the parole board and disappeared just as miraculously after the board had met. They spoke of the danger of "playing games" with God. They showed me the cost of being a Christian in a culture where faith was ridiculed by the power structure and by the community. It was not against the law to be a Christian in prison, but more effective means for discouraging faith exist than mere laws. As a result of the unacceptability of religion, I found in the prison a vibrant faith community in spite of the "persecution" or perhaps because of it. Being Christian had no earthly advantage, but for that reason it was always possible to know why one was a Christian.

For centuries, Christianity has enjoyed most favored religion status in the Western world. People agreed about the basic worldview of Christianity even if they did not accept its faith commitments. Even the person who did not believe in God had the Christian understanding of God in mind when rejecting God. All of that is now rapidly changing. It has not completely changed, but it is changing as a new paganism becomes the worldview of people in the United States. In this situation Christians are hard-pressed to know what to do. The first reaction tends to be the impulse to save the culture. This reaction tends to ignore the fact that modern culture has never been friendly to Christ and his church. It has tolerated the church as the church was willing to become "modern." By and large the church gladly modernized, and in so doing rendered itself no threat at all to the popular culture.

For the time being, people call the emerging new era *postmodernity*. It is a frightening era because all of the rules have changed. To be more precise, there are no rules. All of the old apologetic arguments fall flat because they were developed to address the modern mind-set, which is quickly being replaced by the postmodern mind-set. Rather than panic, however, Christians may find a fresh openness to the gospel, which has not been seen in the West since the Second Great Awakening. Christianity has spent the last two hundred years pointing out the spiritual failings of the modern world. Finally, a generation has appeared that has reacted against the spiritual decay, intellectual stagnation, and artistic mediocrity of modernity to the extent that it has rebelled against modernity's deepest held convictions.

The purpose of this book is to demonstrate how the gospel speaks to the underlying spiritual questions of the emerging postmodern world. In so doing, it will show how the postmodern revolution has swept away many of the greatest barriers to the gospel; such as the old scientific attitude that allowed no place for spiritual reality. The book proceeds from a deep-seated prejudice that only God can bring down a culture. Throughout the Bible we see God raising up and bringing down nations, cultures, and civilizations from the Flood, the Tower of Babel, and Sodom and Gomorrah to Canaan, Israel, and the four great world empires of Daniel. In all situations of major cultural change, God at the same time judges a culture that has failed and creates a situation in which his name may be proclaimed.

TRIUMPH OF THE COUNTERCULTURE

While in Moscow in 1995 I visited the Pushkin Gallery, where I saw an exhibition of Picasso's paintings. I had seen the paintings of Picasso in a dozen American and European galleries, but this exhibition stood out from all the rest. I had seen larger collections, and I had seen more famous paintings by Picasso; but I had never seen a collection that captured the complete chronology of his work from beginning to end. Before my eyes I saw how he had developed as a painter. From year to year, from creative period to creative period, his work changed. As I looked around the room, the collection took on the character of a stop-action movie of a changing landscape from spring to winter.

I saw before my eyes how his painting changed from recognizable forms to cube-shaped figures to erratic lines that suggested what Picasso intended, though the viewer was never quite sure what that might be. This one exhibit captured the cultural history of the twentieth century in art, but it reflected virtually every other realm of knowledge or expression. All the old rules and expectations, the guidelines and norms, the laws and directions, the patterns and customs of culture slowly collapsed. It did not happen suddenly like the collapse of the Berlin Wall, for even the circumstances that led to the fall of the Berlin Wall did not happen suddenly.

Both the United States and China experienced social upheaval in the

1960s. In China the upheaval came as a directive from Mao himself, who provided the movement with the resources and leadership it needed to destroy traditional Chinese culture. The movement was called the Cultural Revolution. In the United States the upheaval arose spontaneously without leadership as much as personalities. It had no clear direction for where it wanted to go. It only intended to leave the old behind. This movement came to be known as the *counterculture*. Mao's movement with its official government sanction failed, but the counterculture in the United States succeeded in scoring a deathblow to any significant presence of tradition in American society.

In 1967 the United States was in ferment. The baby boom generation had started college a few years earlier. Not only did this group represent the largest population pool in American history but it also represented a disproportionately large group of college students, even for its size. A variety of social forces combined to open college to many people who in an earlier time would not have thought of college. State schools heavily subsidized college education, and the federal government made a major investment in state schools to open them up to minority groups and the poor in general. In California, college education came to be regarded as as much of a right and a necessity as public primary and secondary education. In such a climate, college education came virtually free to those who could gain acceptance to a California school. College enrollments soared. College campuses became great hoards of lemmings.

With huge student populations, colleges could no longer exercise the ancient tradition of *in loco parentis*, or operating as the parent of the student while they were in school. The old idea of the college as *alma mater* (foster mother) disappeared except in the more sentimental school songs, which the new glut of students never sang because, due to their unwieldy size, they no longer had occasion to gather in school assemblies. When I started college in 1969, the male curfew had just been abolished but the women still had a curfew. By my sophomore year the administration abolished the offices of dean of men and dean of women. By the time of my graduation the school had open dorms.

During this period, enormous numbers of people came to college unprepared by their parents to live on their own and make life decisions. The World War II generation had raised the baby boomers with one overriding theme in mind: I want my child to have all the things I did not have growing up. As a result, baby boomers had life on a silver platter. They had hula-hoops, Barbie dolls, transistor radios, madras shirts, and English Leather (or "Old Saddle" as my father termed it because he said it smelled like an old saddle). They learned to live from one fad to the next.

To the materialist philosophy that said that my child will be denied nothing, Dr. Spock contributed a radical understanding of child psychology that permeated the raising of children in the fifties and early sixties. Spock taught that children should not be disciplined or prevented from any behavior because the restraint would frustrate them. In essence, Spock encouraged a generation of parents to abdicate the primary responsibility they had for socializing their children. This attitude left a huge group of late adolescents without a road map for navigating life as they went away to college. They were left to experimentation, driven by a lifetime of encouragement to gratify themselves without consideration for other people.

The experimentation expressed itself in the drug culture, the sexual revolution, student demonstrations and riots, unconventional dress, and a total rejection of the values and customs of their parents' generation. The norms of polite society disappeared as the notion of behaving like a gentleman in the presence of a lady became not merely a ludicrous idea, but the essence of what the counterculture hated. Vulgar language became the medium of casual conversation.

The counterculture was not so much about the development of a belief system as it was about leaving Momma and Daddy, not having to go to bed at ten o'clock, not eating any vegetables (which eventually led to not eating any meat for some), and above all, not being someone Momma and Daddy could be proud of. With all of the materialism and indulgence of this generation by their parents, the parents still maintained the "great expectation." They wanted their children to have all that they did not have, but they also wanted their children to be all that they had not become. Their parents had defeated the enemy in the second war to end all wars, so the children refused to fight the little war in Southeast Asia.

Instead of ideology, the counterculture had slogans. These children had not studied Marx and Engels. They had watched TV commercials. Their belief system was all sensory: "If it feels good, do it." Variations included: "Do your own thing," and "Let it all hang out." It was not a very original philosophy. It did not require much thought to understand. All it required was an unrestrained desire for self-gratification. Movies like *Goodbye, Columbus* explored the concept of premarital sex and the idea that abstinence merely prolongs parental control. In the closing scene of the movie, Ali MacGraw's character ends the relationship because her parents found out. Richard Benjamin's character argues that her parents' values do not matter. He demands to know, "But do you think it is wrong?" Hollywood successfully set the agenda for discussion. Sex was not a matter of right and wrong, but of personal preference.

Birth control made free love easy, but not foolproof. Inconvenient pregnancies arose from time to time as a result of casual encounters completely devoid of any sense of commitment. One couple I knew settled the problem by selling their bikes, then reporting them stolen so they could collect the insurance money. With the extra cash she flew to New York and got an abortion without her parents being any wiser. What for centuries had been primarily the problem of the poor and those with "no background" had suddenly become a problem for the children of the middle class. The Supreme Court capitulated to the new social pressure in 1973 and struck down laws against abortion as a violation of a woman's right to control her own body.

Another dimension of the sexual revolution began to appear in the early seventies. As men and women flaunted their sexuality in public orgies, the homosexual community wanted to experience the same sense of freedom. Rejecting the old derogatory terms like *queer* and *fag,* homosexuals adopted the term *gay* to express their sexuality as thousands began to "come out of the closet." From a position of fairness, it seemed only fair that if heterosexuals could do it hanging from the rafters, at least homosexuals should have the freedom to express themselves sexually in public without any social stigma. The fairness argument goes a long way with people who do not want their own freedom for self-gratification restricted. The "*Playboy* philosophy" was expanded to make room for homosexuality because one could not very well view one kind of sexual expression wrong when arguing for complete freedom in sexual experimentation. To say that one thing may be wrong would only open the door to the idea that maybe some other things were wrong as well. Bit by bit the American moral landscape changed. Like the song in *Oklahoma*, it seemed each time they had "gone about as far as they can go."

THE COLLAPSE OF CULTURE

Oswald Spengler described this collapse of culture in *The Decline of the West,* written in the early days of this century. Arnold Toynbee made the same point in the middle of the century with his monumental *A Study of History.* Historians and philosophers have made observations of the phenomenon for centuries. Edward Gibbon's *History of the Decline and Fall of the Roman Empire*, written in the eighteenth century, makes the same point, as does Augustine's fifth-century work *The City of God*: all civilizations collapse. Some last longer than others, but all civilizations collapse.

This phenomenon places Christians in a difficult position. When a culture or civilization begins to collapse, does their first loyalty lie with defending the old order or with advancing the cause of Christ? Unfortunately, when

Christianity holds a preferred place within a culture for a long period of time, Christians have a difficult time distinguishing between the culture and Christian faith. The two become intermingled because people belong to a culture.

The crisis arose for early Christians who had stayed within the Jewish synagogue and continued to worship at the Temple in Jerusalem when the Jewish revolt began in A.D. 68. In that struggle the Christians chose not to revolt against those in authority, but in that choice they made themselves traitors to the old order. To this day, a Jew may be an atheist and find acceptance in the Jewish culture, but a Jew may not be a Christian. Even before the Jewish war, however, the early church began to deal with the problem of cultural differences and how they would affect the church. At the Jerusalem Council mentioned in the book of Acts, the leaders of the church accepted the idea of pluralism within the church. A Jewish church and a Gentile church would exist side by side with different customs, rituals, and values. The willingness of the apostles to accept a Gentile church represented a relativizing of twelve hundred years of Jewish theological tradition. The decision at Jerusalem required the apostles to reflect on the difference between the essence, or eternal truth of their faith, and the external ceremonial forms through which faith expressed itself.

Some Christians tend to think the matter was settled by Constantine, who supposedly made the Roman Empire a Christian nation. While Constantine may have ended the persecution of the Christians, Rome did not cease to have a pagan culture simply because the emperor lifted the persecution. Pagan culture thrived alongside Christianity for more than a hundred years before Augustine wrote *The City of God* to refute the idea that Christianity was to blame for the declining fortunes of the Roman Empire. In this book Augustine laid the intellectual cornerstone of the new culture that began to emerge even as Rome struggled to maintain the old pagan culture. Augustine laid the cornerstone for Christendom, a culture that would thrive for a thousand years until modernity edged it out.

For a thousand years, Western Europe was a politically chaotic region bound together by a common, unifying politicoreligious worldview known as Christendom. The Celtic peoples and their neighbors came to believe in the Creator God who ruled over all people and things, and under whose authority all power is exercised. In the eastern Mediterranean basin, the Eastern Roman Empire or, more popularly, the Byzantine Empire continued to exercise political stability while incorporating the Eastern Church into the official structure of society. Five hundred years of political, linguistic, and cultural separation between the West and the East resulted in different organizational systems for the church, different approaches to biblical interpretation, different worship ceremonies, and different theological explanations of basic Christian doctrine. After 1054 the Eastern Orthodox Church and the Western Roman Catholic Church formally considered each other heretical because of these differences.

Christians have always had a difficult time deciding how close to get to the culture in which they find themselves. Historically this problem emerged most visibly for missionaries, some of whom adopted native dress and others who required their converts to adopt Western dress. Quite subtly, we tend to see some cultures as "Christian" while we label other cultures as pagan. Few people ever recognize the extent to which they equate the way they do things and the things they value as God's final word on the subject. In the nineteenth century this attitude surfaced with the notion that "God is an Englishman!"

In describing the collapse and rise of cultures, modern thinkers like to give a date for the beginning and ending of epochs or cultures. Whereas one may speak fairly authoritatively that Abraham Lincoln lived from 1809 to 1865, one may not make such claims about the life span of a culture. Did Christendom begin with Constantine, Augustus, Gregory the Great, or someone else? Did it end with Martin Luther, the Thirty Years War, the French Revolution, or something else? In fact, most cultural periods overlap, unless all the members of a culture are killed by the succeeding culture. Just as Christendom coexisted with the old pagan culture for many years, modernity coexisted with Christendom for many years. The changes in culture took place so gradually that no one would have noticed except for the occasional military, political, or intellectual battle. One could tell that the thirteenth century was a far cry from the tenth century, but no one noticed much difference between 1034 and 1035. Cultures change. Cultures die. Some cultures are destroyed.

In the last five years the discussion of postmodernity has become a minor industry among Christians and Evangelicals in particular. Books have been written that describe in detail the philosophy of postmodern culture. Thomas Oden dates the beginning of postmodernity with the fall of the Berlin Wall. Others speak of postmodernity as though every person who had a modern worldview had suddenly died so that only people with postmodern views remain to populate the earth. As these commentaries describe in detail the postmodern culture, one is left with the thought that for the first time in history an entire culture has emerged fully formed and universally accepted. Describing the characteristics of baby boomers or generation Xers is one thing, but describing the defining characteristics of the next thousand year epoch as though it is fully formed borders on arrogance. On the other hand, the subject of postmodernity has arisen because culture has begun to change in some perceivable ways. While postmodernity may not yet be an accomplished fact, the changes in contemporary culture relate to a growing rejection of the basic values of modernity.

Because Christianity has continued to exist or coexist with modernity after the collapse of Christendom, many Christians believe that a rejection of the values of modernity means a rejection of the values of Christianity. This assumption would only be valid for those Christians who have compromised their faith to the extent that it has become indistinguishable from the values of modernity. Postmodern thought proceeds from a basic ignorance of Christianity rather than a rejection of it. Modernity rejected Christianity. Whatever the next cultural era will be has not yet developed. The name *postmodern* is no name at all. It only says that something will come next.

Postmodernity represents the period of chaos as modern culture collapses, but it does not yet represent the period of creativity in which the new culture emerges. Because postmodernity represents a rejection of modernity rather than rejection of Christianity, Christians have more to contribute to the definition of the new culture than anyone else. Christians identified the flaws in modernity, which the broader culture has now grown to realize. In this context Christians once again face the dilemma: Will they defend the old order or advance the cause of Christ?

THEOLOGY AND MODERNITY

When Christendom ended, Christians of both liberal and conservative stripe gradually embraced modernity as God's "truth" because it represented their culture. In spite of embracing the new philosophy, however, the majority Christian groups tended to cling to one aspect of Christendom: the union of church and state, which had marked the old Byzantine Empire and Russian Empire in the East and the medieval world in the West. The Lutheran Stats Kirche in Germany, Calvin's Geneva, Puritan England and New England, Catholic Spain and France all represent this tendency to cling to the old era after modernity began to take hold.

Evangelical Christians have long divided between those who took a first-century approach to Christianity and those who took a Christendom approach to Christianity. The first-century Christians believed that society would only change when a sufficient number of people were converted to Christ, the leaven affecting the whole lump of dough. Christendom Christians have tended to act as though society rightfully belongs to Christians and that the laws of the land can create a Christian society. As the fourth great cultural era begins in the West (paganism, Christendom, modernity, postmodernity), many evangelical Christians still look to the attitudes of Christendom to solve the problems of society and to make it reflect Christian values. In seventeenth-century England, the evangelical Christians successfully established a "godly commonwealth" complete with the laws governing behavior that would make the nation pleasing to God. Unfortunately, they failed to convert the next generation, which recalled the king from exile, overthrew the godly laws, and instituted a fierce persecution of nonconformists, which lasted for more than one hundred fifty years.

While clinging to the preference for most-favored religion status within a country, emerging modern theology also reflected a scientific bias, which emerged so gradually that one could hardly notice it. In some sense, Thomas Aquinas in the thirteenth century could be called the father of modern theology. He represented the apex of the intellectual revolution of that period, which has been called the Magnificent Century, a prelude to the Renaissance. His theology is marked by a concern for what people might know because of the existence of a creator God. This approach to theology based on the rediscovered philosophy of Aristotle gave an impetus to what today would be called scientific inquiry; but in the thirteenth century under the influence of Aquinas, all inquiry was theology. With that mind-set, theology came to be regarded as the queen of the sciences. Christendom would crumble as this way of thinking blossomed into the Renaissance and Reformation.

With the reform movements of the sixteenth century, theologians presented new understandings of church organization, worship ceremonies, and doctrinal interpretation. Martin Luther, John Calvin, and Ulrich Zwingli disagreed not only with Rome but with one another. These disagreements led to the great religious wars of the seventeenth century as Lutheran, Reformed, Catholic, and Radical armies fought one another.

The tendency to develop theology on philosophical foundations continued to dominate modern theology. Calvin, a popularizer of Augustine, built his theology on Platonic philosophy. William Perkins, the great English advocate of Reformed theology who gave the Puritan movement its intellectual foundation, built his theology on Ramist philosophy. This approach mirrored the development of modern science, which sought an organizational basis for itself. Theologians sought to discover "spiritual laws" just as scientists sought to discover "natural laws." This discovery of the laws of theology represented a major concern of the Puritans in setting up the new government of England in the Civil War period. At the Westminster Assembly of Divines (1644), which Parliament called to settle the question of religion in England, the first order of business revolved around a discussion of whether or not the Bible contained a rule for the government of the church and, if so, how that rule might be discovered. The Assembly could never reach agreement on the question, and the English church splintered into presbyterian, congregational, and episcopal forms of church government.

Experiences like that of the Puritans led to a movement in theology to establish the scientific study of the Bible. This movement flourished among the Pietists of Germany, led by August Hermann Francke at the University of Halle. Reformed theology took a speculative turn in England and New England, which spawned such views as unitarianism and universalism. Bishop George Berkeley stressed the idea that theology was subject to the laws of scientific observation. In this climate, religious experience came into disfavor as a preference for an intellectual approach to religion prevailed. The supernatural element of religion became discredited as theologians turned instead to a discussion of the moral laws of religion. Deism provided a means of retaining a belief in God without the necessity of retaining belief in the supernatural.

The embracing of modernity occurred in conservative as well as liberal circles. The strategy of modern theology, both conservative and liberal, was to accept the presuppositions of a scientific worldview. In the nineteenth century, the American evangelist Charles Finney established himself as a scholar on the basis of his study of the laws of revival. C. I. Scofield claimed to have developed a "scientific" approach to biblical study at the same time the higher critics of Germany were doing the same thing. Liberal theology retained its allegiance to religious form while rejecting the essence of the Christian faith. Conservative theology, on the other hand, had a preference for reducing the Christian faith to an easily explained formula, repeating the mistake of the scientific method, which tends to observe only what it is looking for.

Rudolf Bultmann conceded the scientific view on miracles, resurrection, and incarnation. He reasoned that since science tells us such things do not happen, the task of New Testament study consists in understanding why the early church would have invented such stories. Karl Barth conceded the scientific view on revelation, thus relativizing the Bible to the same status as all other holy books in the world. No longer was the Bible the word of God. It was now "the word of God for me."

Theologians have always had the danger of confusing theology with the truth. Theology is human thought about God. The word *theology* does not even appear in the Bible, but theology sounds more academic than the word the Bible uses: meditation. All theology is wrong because it involves the human attempt to understand and explain God, but some theology is more wrong than other theology. Christian theology grew too familiar with modernity, such that the old enemy grew into an old friend. Christian theology may have made few converts with its rationalistic arguments in dialogue with modernity, but at least it knew how the conversation went. One of the problems of Christian theology during the modern period was that it matched modern philosophy idea for idea, conceding one major presupposition after another until it looked and sounded like the rest of modernity. With the collapse of modernity and its presuppositions, however, the landscape has changed. People have different views. They do not argue the same way. In fact, they do not want to argue at all.

One group of Christian theologians argues rather vigorously that we should not give up the old theology. The old theology represents their arsenal of weapons against the enemy. Unfortunately, the enemy has changed, and the enemy has a new arsenal of weapons against which the old theology has no effect. It is not ineffective because it is not true, but because it does not aim at the spiritual issues with which the new generation struggles. When Hitler invaded Poland with the most technologically advanced armored cavalry in the world, the Polish cavalry charged Hitler's tanks on horseback. They were not prepared to meet the threat. They were valiant and faithful, but highly ineffective if their commission was to defeat the enemy.

During the Battle of the Bulge, my father fought with the Combat Engineers as Hitler's Panzer divisions drove hard into the Allied lines. Those engineers had no tanks to match the German tanks, but they understood that they did not need to blow up the entire tank to defeat it. They only had to knock out one side of one plate on one track on one side of the tank. They discovered that in their arsenal they had the power to knock out the enemy tanks.

Another group of Christian theologians today advocate embracing the presuppositions of the new postmodern world. On the surface this approach seems to match the enemy weapon for weapon in an intellectual arms race. It actually represents an approach as reactionary as the horse guards. First of all, these theologians begin by conceding the intellectual field just as modern theologians did before them. Then, theology becomes a matter of responding to the agenda of the postmodern mind in kind, or worse, trying to make the Christian faith fit into the worldview of postmodernity.

Theology in the twentieth century became a "discipline" among both conservatives and liberals, practiced by experts in an academic setting. This radical break with the tradition of the church did not happen suddenly; it stood alongside the biblical view of meditation as an alternative since the time of Thomas Aquinas. Great theology, however, requires a ministry context rather than a speculative context. Augustine and Gregory the Great were bishops with specific issues to deal with, which required meditation on the word of God. Gregory of Nazianzus, Basil the Great, and Gregory of Nyssa were all hard-working bishops. Anselm was a hard-working bishop. John Calvin and John Wesley labored in parish ministry. With the dawn of the modern world which began in the late–Middle Ages, theology increasingly came to be viewed as a science in which God became the object of study rather than the teacher. It grew too important to be left to those outside the cloistered halls of learning. Lesslie Newbigin represents a return to the minister-theologian of the Pauline-Petrine-Johannine tradition as the modern paradigm spins into irrelevancy.

CONCLUSION

A wise parent answers the questions a child asks as the child grows up, rather than lecturing the child on what life was like "when I was your age." I wrote my doctoral dissertation on the English Puritans. I have a deep admiration for their love of Scripture, their commitment to the church, and their faithfulness in preaching the gospel to a largely unevangelized nation. I have learned from them, but I also know that their theology spoke to the questions of their day. Postmodernity represents a tragic collection of unanswered questions. The average American today who embraces the postmodern attitudes toward values, spirituality, truth, and consistency has not rejected the biblical meaning of absolute truth. Modern theology speaks of absolute truth as an intellectual concept, when "it" is actually a "he" whose name is Jesus.

One last observation should be made, which deserves a book of its own. Culture in the Middle Ages centered around the tiny part of the population we might call the upper class. During the modern period, culture came under the domination of the middle class. As we move into the future, culture will belong to the widest breadth of people. The counterculture was a movement of white, middle-class kids with the financial resources and time on their hands so that they could afford the luxury of rebellion. In a sense, the counterculture represented the suicide of middle-class domination of Western culture. It had no particular place for most young black Americans who still struggled for a place in the culture against which the leisure class was rebelling. Mass media has had more to do with the spread of the new culture than anything else. Whatever the new postmodern culture will be, however, will only be apparent in the years to come when peoples of color begin to exercise greater influence. For the time, postmodernity remains primarily a white, Western phenomenon—but that is changing.

Christians have the task today of forgetting how they had gone about theology during the modern period, just as the Reformers of five hundred years ago had to forget how theology had been done in Christendom. We must start over very simply with the Bible in hand and listen to the questions the world is asking. The central themes of theology will change, but the gospel will continue to provide the framework for life. Postmodernity as yet lies unfinished. People talk about it and try to describe it, but the most we can say now is that it will be different from modernity. Christians stand in a unique position to direct the next age rather than to fall victim to it.

PART ONE

PERSONALLY FOCUSED

The thirst for personal relationship and the dread of conflict and violence represent the driving themes of the postmodern generation. These two issues work themselves out in terms of the preference for personal rather than institutional involvement, a preference for acceptance of all differences rather than conflict over differences, and a desire for a sense of wholeness in a fragmented world.

In a highly mobile society accompanied by the breakdown of the extended family as well as of the traditional family unit, relationship has become an increasingly valuable commodity because it is so difficult to obtain and maintain. The postmodern age is an anonymous age with a yearning for relationship. Existential isolation has come to full flower as people seek relationship through joining formal small groups and develop anonymous relationships over the Internet. People will talk about emotions, feelings, failures, dreads, aspirations, and inadequacies before perfect strangers in a plea for attention and caring relationship.

In this climate, the central Christian teaching of a God who made himself manifest in human form in order to seek relationship with people stands in stark contrast to the kind of impersonal deity of Eastern religion or the judgmental and condemning God of Islam. The Incarnation was an embarrassment to the modern age, but it makes good sense to an age dying for meaningful relationship.

Christianity has no special status in the postmodern age, but it is as valid as any other worldview and worthy of exploring. Pluralism finally frees Christianity from cultural domination to an extent it has not enjoyed in the

West since the great persecution under the Emperor Diocletian. In a "Christian culture" everyone is a "Christian"; therefore, nothing is expected other than assent. No sense of urgency pervades the church. The concerns tend to be parochial and sectarian in nature. After the success of the counterculture, Christianity lost its respectability in the major cultural centers of the United States.

As this trend increases, Christianity must return to the gospel in order to gain adherents. Christianity can offer no other advantages in postmodernity than Christ himself. While pluralism offers a great opportunity for Christians to return to the gospel as their primary point of orientation, the danger remains that Christians will pursue an ethnic response to pluralism and withdraw to themselves in order to preserve a peculiar cultural orientation to their faith.

Postmodernity has rejected the segmentation of knowledge and the segmentation of experience. Integration and holistic thinking have become hallmarks of the emerging postmodern mind. The church in the West adopted modernity's segmentation and specialization wholeheartedly in the organization of theological education and the administration of denominational bureaucracy. The Academy has the tendency to regard the way it does things as *the* way to do things.

Christianity has the opportunity to show people in the postmodern age what it means to experience peace, *shalom*, not as the world gives, but as only God can give. This wholeness that affects every aspect of life has not been particularly visible in the Christianity of modernity, but those closets of Christianity that are wed to modernity will die out.

CHAPTER ONE

I'LL GET BY WITH A LITTLE HELP FROM MY FRIENDS: RELATIONSHIP

Twenty years ago I sat in an oak-lined room on a heavily padded blue leather davenport before a huge fireplace in Oxford. There I talked late into the night with a man who was looking for something. A self-made millionaire, he had retired from a career on Madison Avenue at the age of forty in order to devote himself to the search. Jewish by heritage but not by practice, his family had fled to Australia from Central Europe in the mid-1930s to escape Hitler. His parents died in Australia when he was still quite young.

In his search, he had gone to Israel. Something about the place told him that "it" really could be found, but he did not find it. He spent time in the South of France where he heard a man speaking at a conference in a hotel where he was staying. He decided that the man knew what it was he was searching for. He followed the speaker back to Oxford where he taught and presided over one of the smaller colleges of the university. Being a brilliant man, he enrolled in the professor's college, and there we met. We got to be friendly; but he warned me that when I left, he would not be there to say good-bye. If I wrote to him, he would not answer my letters.

Late into that particular night we talked about religion in general and the God of the Christians in particular. He did not know why Christians spoke so much about the love of Jesus. He did not consider Jesus to be such a loving figure. On the contrary, he considered Jesus rather austere and remote. He wanted to know what Jesus meant by love. Since he commanded his disciples to love, was love just ethics? Then he said that he could not love a

God who would let his own son be killed, even for him. That would be like a father who threw his child in front of a bus. What kind of God is that?

The man I met at Oxford is only one of countless millions who miss something they have never experienced. They only know it exists because of the longing they feel for it. This longing, this poverty, provides the driving force behind what many people call postmodernity. On the surface, the postmodern generation has a fixation with personal experience, but it goes deeper than mere subjectivity. They focus on the personal rather than the intellectual because they feel the greatest loss at the personal level. They miss something personal, something relational; but they do not know what it is.

HOW DID WE GET IN THIS FIX?

For centuries, Christendom was marked as a time of sedentary lifestyles; people lived in the same place. For nearly a thousand years, people lived in the same place. Generation after generation lived in the same village. Peasants were bound to the land and to their feudal relationships to the lord of the manor who in turn owed obligations of protection to them. Christendom was marked by relationships. Each community had a parish church, which formalized the communal relationship where all came to worship under one roof. The sense of community was very important during the period of Christendom.

With the dawn of the modern age, all of that changed. The Enclosure Act in England and Scotland resulted in a change of how the land was used. Until then a number of peasants worked small farms for the great landowner. When the English economy changed and the great landowners realized there was more money to be made in sheep and wool, they dispossessed the peasants and enclosed the fields for sheep. The nobles did not need as many peasants working the land, and as a result the peasants had no place to go but to the towns. This migration marked the beginning of the growth of cities in England and in Europe, as well as the beginning of industrialization. It also marked the end of what has been called the Social Contract and community relationships. The cities had no Social Contract. People did not have the same kinds of relationships and support systems in the cities. People were taken out of their traditional relationships and out of their family heritage when they moved to the cities.

This changing nature of society, this dislocation, this breaking of relationships and the resulting social problems was a major concern of many social commentators from the beginning of the modern period. John Bunyan in *Pilgrim's Progress* comments on some of the problems in towns that resulted from people no longer having a place to work, no longer being on the farm. Jonathan Swift and Daniel Defoe wrote about it in the 1700s in some of their scandalous novels that described immorality in the city of London. Charles Dickens wrote about it in the nineteenth century. He wrote about the workhouses and the squalor in the slums of London. Many of the fictional characters in these stories had been dispossessed of the land and had no place to go.

Then the political philosophers Engels, Hegel, and Marx wrote about the problem of workers being separated from nature and no longer being able to enjoy the fruit of their labor. The workers labored for someone else, who derived the profit. This was the beginning of socialism and communism as the solution to the breakdown in relationship, the alienation from nature, and the alienation from other people. People like Kierkegaard carried it one step further and spoke about one's own alienation from oneself, and the term "existentialism" came into being. One aspect of existentialism involves the isolation of people who feel cut off from others, cut off from themselves, and cut off from God. It is a problem that is most apparent in an urban context.

In the United States, rural life characterized this country for well into the second half of its existence. Even into this century, rural life was, for the first half of this century, the standard for people in the United States. Thomas Jefferson had an ideal of a nation of yeoman farmers. He held that "the city is a pox on the body politic." The importance of communities, relationships, and neighbors could not be overstated for Jefferson in terms of a healthy society. Jefferson did not speak from a Christian perspective, but he understood the issue from a political philosopher's perspective.

The "me first" generation does not represent an entirely new trend in the United States. Rugged individualism has always formed a part of the American identity. When I was in the second grade, I learned that Abraham Lincoln's father believed that when he could see the smoke from his neighbor's chimney, it was time to move.

With the industrial revolution, however, we saw entire communities uprooted. People migrated in search of jobs. Especially during the Great Depression, huge migrations took place. People left the rural South of Mississippi and Alabama to go north to Detroit looking for jobs. People left the Appalachian Mountains to go to Ohio and Pittsburgh looking for jobs in the steel and rubber industries. People left Oklahoma and the plains to go to California looking for jobs. We saw three major migrations in the middle of this century: the Depression migration followed by World War II, a second migration related to the war industry and a reshuffling of jobs, followed by a third migration in the 1950s as people coming back from World War II continued to look for new opportunities.

With all of that going on, we saw the development of urban blight in the United States as we had not known it before. There had always been problems in the larger cities, but nothing like we have seen since the 1950s. Traffic, crime, and pollution exploded. We have seen conflict between the inner cities and the suburbs. Continuing political battles occur in metropolitan areas over where the financial resources go. The big money may be made in the inner city in the high-rise office buildings, yet the people who work there flee to the suburbs in the evening and take their salaries with them. The tax money goes to the suburban communities and not to the cities and that creates conflict and alienation between the urban dwellers and the suburban dwellers. We have seen racial strife in the 1950s, '60s, '70s, '80s and '90s. We have seen fear of other races lead to hatred of other races, leading to violence. All of this turmoil leads to a violation of relationships.

WHERE ARE WE TODAY?

We continue to have a mobile society. The average American moves every three years. This statistic seemed outrageous to me. I could not believe Americans moved so often, until I realized that I have moved every three years. As a result of this sort of movement, the average American no longer has an extended family. They may know of relatives they have, but the children do not know cousins. They do not know aunts and uncles. They do not know grandparents. They may know of them and may have visited them from time to time, but they do not know them. They do not know them well enough to climb up on the grandparents' knees and hug them and talk. They are strangers. As a result of this moving around, people lack the kind of cultural identity that would come from the tradition and heritage of a place.

I grew up in one place, and I drank deeply of what it meant to be from Greenville, South Carolina. I knew the stories and the history and the old heroes of Greenville and the state of South Carolina. My daughters have lived in Kentucky, Minnesota, and Tennessee; and I have noticed that my daughters fiercely say "I'm from Kentucky" no matter where we happen to be living. Kentucky is their state, and they are working to maintain an identity as Kentuckians. My wife and I work hard to continue to make that possible. We make trips back to Louisville regularly, every couple of months. It is important for them; and as long as they realize they are from Kentucky, we want to strengthen that sense of identity. But most people do not have that sense of being related to people in a given place. The latchkey generation is coming of age in a country where one of two marriages ends in divorce. Thus, stable relationship is something that this generation has grown up unaccustomed to experiencing. They even lack lasting friendships because moving as frequently as they do, they must continually make new short-term friends. I can call my friend Hank Harrison on the telephone; and we can talk for an hour, picking up where we left off six months or a year ago because we started the first grade together. My daughters do not have those kinds of relationships. The postmodern generation does not know that kind of stability. As a result, they crave relationship.

Loneliness is very serious. In God's first observation of his creature he said, "It is not good for the man to be alone" (Gen 2:18). Relationship is a fundamental, absolute need of people. Loneliness is destructive to us. It destroys us. Part of the gift of salvation in the gospel, if not the very gift, is relationship. Salvation is not a commodity that you hold on to. Salvation is the Savior himself who comes and makes his home with us and creates a relationship. One of our greatest opportunities is not offering an organization, but offering ourselves, which is sometimes a scary thing to do for an older generation that has survived by keeping other people at arm's distance.

Oddly enough, people who feel trapped in a crowd sometimes seek isolation instead of the very relationship they crave. It is something that demographers have already noticed with the West Coast. People are leaving California. They are going to Idaho, Montana, Colorado, Oregon, and Washington. They are leaving, and they are opting to give up income. They are choosing to do with less financially in order to have a simpler lifestyle. This is possible for people in a certain financial status. Many people are in a position to choose to slow down and do with less. The people who need it the most, however, often do not have the option. Part of the question that we have to deal with is not just how we take care of our own families, but what do we about the masses of people who are trapped in the cities. Who is bringing the gospel there and how is it coming? These are relational issues. In some cases these are generational matters in the choice of loneliness or isolation, but it does something to a person. There is a toll. Some people choose to pay the price; such is the hermit. It is possible to be a hermit in a neighborhood such that one neighbor does not know who the other neighbors are. But it still takes a toll on us. It is not good that we are alone. It is destructive to us.

Most churches in the United States since World War II have been big meetings. That is, you go to the big meeting, listen to the lecture, and then you leave. There is no real connection with the people in the room with you. Other kinds of churches exist. Some churches grow around small groups or Sunday school, which fosters relationships. But that is almost a peculiarity of the South, which has become a standing joke among evangelicals. You find small groups in other parts of the country, but it is not the norm. I did not realize until I spent time in Minnesota that the average church does not have small groups for adults. We have a pattern in the United States in which churches regard Sunday school as "kids' stuff" and home Bible studies as too much trouble. Relationship building has not been a major agenda item embraced by the church in the United States as a whole. There are exceptions; but as a whole, churches are places of isolation. Without this relational dimension at its core, the church looks like just another organization or civic club to the postmodern generation.

The postmodern generation will not visit the church building. They will not go to the lecture. They will not join the organization. The church looks like just one more institution. They are interested not in institutions but in relationships. We have to go to them. For them to listen to us, the sharing of the gospel has to take place in a relational way, that is, a conversation. An interesting study was conducted a few years ago by Kirk Hadaway and Penny Marler, two sociologists who happen to be Christians.[1] They were concerned with the phenomenon of Americans indicating their religious preference in surveys. Most people in the United States will put something down. The Gallup poll and other sociological studies have reported for years that 40 percent of the people in the United States are in church every Sunday. Every pastor knows that statistic; and every pastor also knows, of course, that it holds true in every other community except their own, which they view as abnormal. Marler and Hadaway decided that since every pastor they knew lived in an abnormal community, perhaps the figure needed checking. They studied the figure more closely and discovered that Americans lie, which should not come as a surprise. Actually, less than 20 percent of the people in the United States go to church on Sunday.

The same Americans who say "I voted" and did not will say "I go to church" and do not. They still are holding on to some childhood training that says you ought to go to church on Sunday. So, of course, they say they go to church on Sunday, just not this Sunday. Marler and Hadaway wanted to understand what people mean in a poll when they say "I am Presbyterian" or "I am Christian." What they mean is their family has always been Presbyterian. They mean that as opposed to Catholic, they are Protestant. They mean that they are American, and Americans have been always been sort of Christian; so they are Christian. As it turns out, the religious self-identification meant very little at all.

Marler and Hadaway discovered something else in conducting this study in which they talked with about 2,500 people. They discovered that everybody will talk about religion, often in intimate terms, the same way that people will get on the *Oprah Winfrey Show* and talk about their deepest concerns. People do the same thing on the Internet in chat groups and have on-line conversations about matters of intimate concern. Very few people want to be lectured to either about flossing their teeth, or voting, or going to church, or polishing their shoes, or getting saved. Americans do not like to be lectured to, but they love to talk. What Marler and Hadaway discovered was that people would go into detail about their own experiences, about why they do not like church, about what someone said to them, about what happened to their parents, about relationships with a spouse, or about their children and the trouble they are in. They would go into deep, personal, intimate details.

If you have a basis for relationship, you have a basis for meaningful conversation. The implication for how we do apologetics and evangelism is something Oscar Thompson talked about more than twenty years ago. You work within your existing relationships. That is your mission field. You express care and concern, and you modify your approach. Rather than giving the lecture, maybe just listen a little more. The more they will tell you, the more you can understand how Jesus Christ is the solution to the problem they are experiencing. I am very simplistic at this point; I believe Jesus is the answer. Then the problem becomes understanding the question on someone's mind. Only then can I show someone how Jesus addresses their ultimate problem.

THE INCARNATION

The Christian faith does not deal primarily with the forms of religion. Christianity takes many different forms in different cultures. It has tremendous flexibility because it is not primarily about its form. It is about a personal relationship with God. Not all spirituality is based on this idea. In fact, it is quite unusual among the religions of the world.

The idea of the divine having anything to do with the physical world would have been disturbing to the Greeks of the first century. The Gospel of John declared of the Word:

> He was in the world, and though the world was made through him, the world did not recognize him. He came to that which was his own, but his own did not receive him. Yet to all who received him, to those who believed in his name, he gave the right to become children of God—children born not of natural descent, nor of human decision or a husband's will, but born of God.
>
> The Word became flesh and made his dwelling among us. We have seen his glory, the glory of the One and Only, who came from the Father, full of grace and truth. (John 1:10-14)

This declaration constituted the truly radical moment. This assertion was the great stumbling block: the idea that God had entered into creation. John insisted that God, who was perfect, holy, unapproachable, totally removed from sin, totally different from creation had come into creation. He had not just come into creation to look around, but had experienced what it means to be human! By experiencing it he laughed, he cried, he hungered, he tired, and he experienced it to the point that he could be nailed on a cross and killed.

Think what it would mean if you had always viewed the physical world as something that God or the Spirit not only would not have anything to do with but could not have anything to do with. Then, all of a sudden, you are told that God came into this world and took on flesh. That view of God is the basis of the Christian message, and it was repulsive to the Greek philosophers who on Mars Hill told Paul he was crazy. It was repulsive to the Jews who had the idea of a God so holy and so unapproachable that they even stopped saying his name. When he came to Moses and called him to lead Israel, he said, "Moses, my name is Yahweh. 'I am who I am' " (from Exod. 3:14). Yet, they felt that God was so unapproachable that when God spoke to them from the mountain, they said in effect, "Moses you go talk to him. We don't want to talk to him. It's too scary" (see Exod. 20:19). God sent prophets to speak to Israel because they were afraid to hear his voice, and through the years they pushed God further and further and further away. By the time of Jesus, whenever they found the holy name written in the Hebrew scriptures they did not say his name, they said, "the LORD." To say that the Lord, the one that only the high priest could approach and then only once a year within the Holy of holies of the Temple, had come in the flesh was truly shocking.

On the other hand, there is an incredible beauty to the idea of the Creator coming into creation. Bishop Stephen Neill, who for many years was a missionary in India, said that God did not just create this world and leave it, but that he loved us enough to come into it. The old Native American expression "walk a mile in our moccasins" suggests the significance of God sharing human existence. The one who created us is sympathetic with us. The book of Hebrews contains the great teaching that because Jesus Christ came into this world, we have a sympathetic High Priest. Have you ever been in a situation when somebody was going through a great difficulty and you said, "I know how you feel." Only, you really didn't because you had never been through that kind of situation. I think one of the most comforting things about the Christian faith is to know that when I die I will be embraced and kept from death by somebody who knows what it means to die. And because he knows what it means to die, I will never find out what it means to die. He knows what it means to be tempted, so he wants to help me when I am tempted. That is his desire. We have a sympathetic God. That's amazing and it's radical. In the history of religion in the world, there is nothing else quite like it. Instead of form and institutions, Jesus Christ offers relationship with himself.

BACK TO THE FUTURE

Christians dealing with a major shift in culture like that which appears to be happening with the postmodern generation have the tremendous advantage of the experience of Christians who have gone through such times before. The apostles had to make such a shift when they left the culture of old Israel to bring the gospel message to the pagan world of the Gentiles. The apostles agreed that the Gentiles did not need to adopt the culture of the Jews to be saved, but they did need to know the Savior. The Gospel of John especially captures the principles of communicating the gospel with people with whom we share few if any common values. At the heart of the communication of the gospel lies the teaching of Jesus about the role of a witness who gives personal testimony about him. From the beginning, faith in Jesus was meant to be both personal and relational.

John wrote his Gospel to talk about the personal God who came into the world to relate to people. As soon as he has described the kind of God he intends to talk about, he begins to describe the personal experiences of people. He starts with the experience of John the Baptist. John the Baptist was the cousin of Jesus of Nazareth and one of the most important and influential preachers of his day. He was executed by King Herod for his religious beliefs.

John's testimony was this: "The next day John saw Jesus coming toward him and said, 'Look, the Lamb of God, who takes away the sin of the world' " (John 1:29). John the Baptist equated Jesus with the total sacrificial system of the Old Testament. He is the fulfillment of all of the sacrificial laws in the book of Leviticus. He is the fulfillment of everything that the Law of Moses said concerning sacrifice, atonement, and salvation from sin. He is the fulfillment of everything that the Temple was established to do. He is the fulfillment of the Passover. He is all of the religion of Israel wrapped into one person. A person replaces the forms and institutions of religion.

Then John the Baptist elaborated: "This is the one I meant when I said, 'A man who comes after me has surpassed me because he was before me.' I myself did not know him, but the reason I came baptizing with water was that he might be revealed to Israel" (John 1:30-31). First of all he says, "he was before me." In Luke 1:13, 18-19, 24-27 we find the story of how John the Baptist was born. Luke tells how John was conceived and how the angel appeared to his father and said, "Your wife is going to have a baby, and you will call his name John." The father did not believe it was going to happen, so he was struck speechless until the child was born. The neighbors asked, "Well, what are you going to name him? Can you scratch it out or something?" When he finally indicated the name would be John, he could speak again.

The interesting thing is that John was born before Jesus. John was conceived six months before Jesus was conceived. Yet, John says, "He was before me." When John was in his mother's womb, we are told by Luke, Mary went to visit her cousin Elizabeth. When she entered the room, the Holy Spirit came upon Elizabeth and that little baby in her womb, and that little baby leaped for joy in the presence of this yet unborn Jesus. John was filled with the spirit from the womb, but Jesus was different. Jesus was conceived of the Holy Spirit.

THE TESTIMONY OF THE HOLY SPIRIT

John the Baptist bore witness that Jesus was before him. Jesus is the Lamb of God; and the very reason John was baptizing was so that it could be revealed to Israel who the Messiah, the promised one, was going to be. John gave this testimony, "I saw the Spirit come down from heaven as a dove and remain on him. I would not have known him, except that the one who sent me to baptize with water told me, 'The man on whom you see the Spirit come down and remain is he who will baptize with the Holy Spirit.' I have seen and I testify that this is the Son of God" (John 1:32-34).

We are told by John the apostle that when Jesus came to his people, they did not know him. John the Baptist also said that he was one of the ones who did not know Jesus. He had known him all of his life. He was his cousin, but he did not know who Jesus really was until at the baptism. Mark described it as though the heavens were torn apart like cloth being ripped and the Spirit descended upon Jesus. John had been waiting. We do not know how long; but since the beginning of his ministry when he started baptizing, he was waiting for something to happen. God had revealed to him that in baptizing God would reveal the one that he had promised for centuries and centuries. So John says that the Spirit revealed who Jesus was.

Now, it is important to see that God had prepared John the Baptist ahead of time to receive the message. John the Baptist is not the only one in human history whom God has prepared ahead of time to receive a message. Regardless of whether persons become a Christian as a tiny child, as a teenager, or as an adult, God prepares them before anyone tells them about Jesus. God's Spirit was at work preparing John to receive a most miraculous and dramatic thing. The Spirit bore witness that Jesus was the Christ, and we find this witness and confirmation not only in John's Gospel but also in Luke, Mark, and Matthew. That is one matter about which they all commented. John often talks about things that the other Gospels do not mention. Here is a point that they all wanted to be sure everybody understood, because God had revealed Jesus as his Son through his Spirit at the baptism.

The anointing by the Spirit of God at the baptism began the public ministry of Jesus. It did not mark the beginning of Jesus being the Son of God. Jesus was the Son of God before the baptism. The Holy Spirit and Jesus were together before the baptism. The Holy Spirit did not come to Jesus for the first time at the baptism. That is why John begins his Gospel by explaining that the Word was one with God at the beginning. The anointing at the baptism is a different kind of experience. The British Royal Family gives us a glimpse of what was happening at the baptism of Jesus. Some years ago, Queen Elizabeth took her eldest son to Wales to the ruins of Caernarvon Castle; and there on television and with the nobility of the realm surrounding her, Prince Charles knelt before her. She took a little crown, a coronet, placed it on his head, and declared him publicly the Prince of Wales. The investiture began his formal life of service. At the baptism, Jesus was publicly declared by the Father to be the Son; and the manifestation of the Holy Spirit was the sign to John the Baptist of who Jesus was. John believed because of the testimony of the Holy Spirit.

THE IMPORTANCE OF TESTIMONY

Testimony is very important. Testimony is the essential method of communicating faith in the New Testament. In the twentieth century Christians developed all kinds of gimmicks and plans for doing evangelism, but John is vitally concerned with the whole idea of testimony. Giving testimony is why he wrote his book. In explaining why he wrote his Gospel, John said, "Jesus did many other miraculous signs in the presence of his disciples, which are not recorded in this book. But these are written that you may believe that Jesus is the Christ, the Son of God, and that by believing you may have life in his name" (John 20:30-31). Then later he remarked, "This is the disciple who testifies to these things and who wrote them down. We know that his testimony is true. Jesus did many other things as well. If every one of them were written down, I suppose that even the whole world would not have room for the books that would be written" (John 21:24-25). Not only in his Gospel but also in the first letter of John, he stressed the compulsion to give testimony about what he knew from his own experience:

That which was from the beginning, which we have heard, which we have seen with our eyes, which we have looked at and our hands have touched—

this we proclaim concerning the Word of life. The life appeared; we have seen it and testify to it, and we proclaim to you the eternal life, which was with the Father and has appeared to us. We proclaim to you what we have seen and heard, so that you also may have fellowship with us. And our fellowship is with the Father and with his Son, Jesus Christ. We write this to make our joy complete. (1 John 1:1-4)

Finally, when a very old man and slave on the island of Patmos, John received a revelation. He wrote again about the importance of testimony in the opening verses of Revelation: "The revelation of Jesus Christ, which God gave him to show his servants what must soon take place. He made it known by sending his angel to his servant John, who testifies to everything he saw—that is, the word of God and the testimony of Jesus Christ" (Rev. 1:1-2).

Testimony is crucially important, but the remarkable thing about the testimony that Christians give about their own experience of Jesus Christ is that the Holy Spirit does the same thing for them and their testimony that he did for John two thousand years ago. That is, the Holy Spirit is the *other* witness. In ancient Israel, it took two witnesses to confirm and verify the truth. The New Testament speaks of this custom in many places, but one of the promises to Christians is that the Spirit bears witness with them and that conversion to faith in Christ does not simply depend upon techniques. Ultimately, it depends upon how the Holy Spirit takes all our failures, misspoken words, stutters, illogical skipping from one point to another, and miraculously brings it to a person. The Holy Spirit takes it to the heart of another person and confirms the truth.

The Gospel of John reveals how things two thousand years ago make a difference today, and how the miraculous work of God in the world two thousand years ago is still going on today. Recognizing this reality involves remembering what God has done and opening our eyes to notice what the Lord is still doing. Recovering the personal, relational approach to faith found in the New Testament provides the basis for understanding how to share the gospel of Christ with a postmodern generation that is more interested in relationship than institutions.

REPRISE

Twenty years ago as I talked late into the night, I heard a lonely man saying he wanted nothing to do with a God who would kill his own son. I heard a man saying he understood nothing about the personal, intimate nature of God. I heard a man saying he could not fathom the meaning of love. I heard a man saying he was afraid to experience the one thing he wanted most in life. I heard a man saying that he projected all the violence of humanity onto God.

He heard Christians say, "For God so loved the world that he gave his only begotten son." He heard Christians say that God killed Jesus. He is not alone. A growing movement of feminists also reject any meaningful atoning death of Jesus because they understand it to mean that God wanted blood. These views have more to do with how people have experienced life than with anything they may have gained from studying Scripture. This view is largely an emotional response to pain.

As my arm-length friend said that the death of Jesus was like a father who threw his child in front of a bus, I heard myself responding almost out of body. I said, "No, it's like a father who sees his child wandering out into the street, ignorant that a bus is bearing down on him; and the father rushes out to push the child out of the way only to be struck by the bus himself, because *God was in Christ reconciling the world unto himself.*" It was a strange experience for me, because I had never memorized that verse of Scripture. It was strange also because I had never fully grasped the meaning of the Incarnation of God in Christ.

People searching for ultimate personal experience and fulfillment will only find one religion that teaches about a God who so loves people that he would identify with them completely, even to the point of experiencing death with them. A personal, self-conscious God who created the physical and the spiritual worlds makes meaning and purpose a possibility. Without such a being, everything is an accident of gigantically improbable proportions. With such a God, however, people can find fulfillment, meaning, and the possibility of genuine relationships with others, because that God came into the world to bring people to himself and through that relationship to bring people together.

My experience in that conversation with the man in Oxford also taught me something about the nature of revelation and the Holy Spirit. A personal God has relationship with people and communicates with them. The reliability of Scripture finds confirmation in the personal nature of God. A personal God would communicate. The fact that Scripture came over centuries demonstrates the ongoing interest of God with people. That night in Oxford, however, I was as much in communication with God as I was with the man I saw. The Holy Spirit of God relates to people personally, not as a mere "force" or power. The Holy Spirit taught me things that night about God as he brought from the hidden recesses of my mind a verse of Scripture which I had heard but which had never made an impact on me before.

CHAPTER TWO

LIVE AND LET LIVE: PLURALISM

Christendom had a monolithic value and belief system that stretched all across Europe until an October day in 1517 when a German monk and theology professor tacked a notice on the door of the castle church in Wittenberg announcing that he wanted to debate ninety-five ideas he thought needed reforming in the church. That sparked the Protestant Reformation, which broke up the monolithic value system of Europe or Christendom as it was then.

A culture is defined in terms of the commonly held beliefs, practices, and attitudes of the people within it. In his monumental study of civilization, Arnold Toynbee concluded that religion was the most important aspect of every culture. The princely rulers of Europe understood this dynamic. In the bridge time between Christendom and modernity, they understood the role that religion played in holding a society together or in tearing it apart.

During the late Middle Ages in southern France, a heretical religious group developed called the Albigensians or the Cathari. They had a mixture of Christian ideas and the ancient Manichaean ideas of dualism between physical and spiritual, the physical being evil and the spiritual being good. This major heresy quickly spread in the southern area of France, and the Pope called for a crusade to suppress this heresy. The princely rulers of Europe gladly joined in to be sure that it did not spread. A great war ensued in which the Albigensians were wiped out. This crusade initiated the idea of an inquisition in Europe to deal with aberrations or differences in religious thinking or religious practice. The most famous inquisition took place in Spain. It was initiated by Ferdinand and Isabella in the year that Christopher Columbus set sail for China. As a result of that inquisition, the Muslims and the Jews were expelled from Spain.

When Martin Luther began the controversy that resulted in the Protestant Reformation, the Holy Roman Emperor grew quite alarmed. He was concerned with how differences in religion might affect his very fragile empire. It was an empire of different languages and different ethnic groups spread across Europe, and he wanted just one religion in his empire. Of course, he had his own religious piety; but he had his political concerns to think of as well. The German princes, on the other hand, had other considerations, such as the growing concern for their autonomy over their own independent state. Though they wanted to separate from the empire, they too wanted just one religion within their domain. When the religious wars of the Protestant Reformation were over, the peace settlement included the stipulation that the religion of the prince of a domain would be the religion of the people. If the prince was Lutheran, then the state church of that domain would be Lutheran. If the prince was Reformed or Calvinistic, then the state religion of that domain would be the Reformed church. In Bavaria, the state church became Catholic; in Brandenburg, that state church became Protestant. There was diversity, but to a limited extent. The total culture of Western Europe was beginning to fragment.

Henry VIII had the same concern in England. He made himself the head of the church in England, which was a further fragmentation of allegiance to Rome. He wanted no outside interference in his country, which had been a long-standing tradition of monarchs in England. The English kings had actually been striving with the Pope since the time of King John in the late 1100s and early 1200s. Henry's daughter, Elizabeth, who became queen in 1558, made it quite clear that she wanted no further reformation of the church in England. The Church of England would retain many of the old customs of the English church, but they would not move toward a more thorough reformation of the ceremonies and the practices. Elizabeth expected conformity to the established church, and she would allow no diversity. The Puritans at this time were the ones crying for more freedom in worship. They also wanted to dispense with such things as robes and vestments, candles, and the altar against the east wall rather than a table at the crossing of the parish church. They wanted to do away with many of the symbols, but Elizabeth would allow for no diversity because diversity was dangerous to the unity of the state and the solidarity of the culture.

When he came to the throne after the great English Civil War, Charles II enacted the Clarendon Code, which persecuted the nonconformists. The state enforced conformity to the Church of England, and those who did not conform could not go to universities, could not hold office, and could be jailed for violations of the terms of conformity. John Bunyan spent a number of years in jail for violating the terms of conformity. He preached without a license.

Louis XIII in France, though Catholic and though recognizing the Pope, still wanted authority over the Catholic Church in France. He began a movement known as the Gallican Movement after the ancient name, Gaul, for the area of France. It involved the idea of establishing a truly Gallican church. Through association with the power structure of France and subservience to the monarchy, the French church, in the popular view of the people, was weakened by association with the monarchy. When the French Revolution came, the republic that was set up became an atheistic republic. It was a republic that was tired of the church. The church in France was seen to be dispensable or not necessary for a country.

As a result of the American Revolution and the establishment of the American republic, the Baptists had the opportunity to influence Congress to pass an amendment to the Constitution that guaranteed the separation of church and state. This amendment declared that Congress shall make no laws respecting the establishment of religion or denying the free exercise of religion. Thomas Jefferson was one of the founding fathers most sympathetic to that idea. Jefferson said "I have sworn on the altar of God eternal hostility toward every form of tyranny over the minds of men." This famous declaration did not refer to the tyranny of the British government. Rather, he was talking about the tyranny of the Episcopal Church, the state church of Virginia, which is to say that he declared war on the state church. He did not rest until the establishment of a state church was abolished in Virginia. The Baptists applauded that action because they had spent time in jail for not conforming to the state church of Virginia.

Early in the history of this country Christians accepted pluralism because it provided protection to the religious groups from each other. The colonies that became states were largely ethnic groups unto themselves. New Jersey was a Swedish Lutheran colony. New York was a Dutch Reformed colony. Pennsylvania was an English colony, but a Quaker colony. Maryland was an English colony, but a Catholic colony. Massachusetts was an English colony, but a Congregational colony. Rhode Island was an English colony, but it was an open colony founded on the principle of religious toleration or pluralism. The southern colonies were English colonies, but they were largely economic colonies. They were founded by companies designed to make money. They were a mixed bag to begin with, especially colonies like North Carolina,

South Carolina, and Georgia, which had people from Germany, France, England, Scotland, and Wales, all representing different churches.

Early on there was a commitment in this nation to pluralism based on self-interest. The Baptists no longer had to fear the Episcopalians, and the Lutherans no longer had to fear the Presbyterians and the Congregationalists. But pluralism meant Protestant pluralism. It did not mean general religious toleration, it meant Protestant pluralism. Jews and Catholics still tended to be second-class citizens until World War I. Though Congress could make no laws respecting the establishment of religion, there were ways at the local and state level to ensure the Protestant ascendancy. During most of the republic, Christianity enjoyed most-favored religion status, though unofficially and without government connection. It was a cultural matter. The United States, culturally, was a Christian nation.

This cultural Christianity, this general sense that America was a Christian nation such that at wartime we would sing songs like "God Bless America," and this general acknowledgment that we were "one nation, under God" came to an end in 1963 with the Supreme Court decision concerning prayer and devotions in local schools. The decision was that local school boards could not prescribe set prayers to be said in school. It did not abolish prayer in school, but it said that the local school board could not write a prayer that everyone would say. Though the Supreme Court did not go that far, in practice across the country prayer and devotional readings left the public schools. School boards, principals, and teachers did not want to deal with the issue. The public schools had been the means of making Christianity the cultural religion. It was the way of carrying on the tradition. This situation does not mean that people were Christians as a result of being in public school. It meant they were aware of the Christian tradition. That awareness began to disappear very quickly after 1963. The schools had been the primary agent for transferring the worldview from one generation to the next. It was the idea that if I was an atheist in the United States, the God I did not believe in was the God of the Bible. Even those who did not have faith defined their infidelity in terms of the Christian faith. That was the worldview and if I did not participate in that, it was still my worldview that I was not participating in. Generally, the culture as a whole had one concept of God, whether they believed in God or not. They had one basic concept of right or wrong such that if they chose not to do right, they knew they were choosing not to do right and that what they were doing was considered wrong, but it was their choice.

As a result of the schools no longer being the place for passing on the cultural tradition, the baby buster generation that started in 1963, grew up without the basic exposure to biblical categories and values that previous generations had been aware of. This religious exposure was not instruction in the Christian faith, but it was a general informing of a tradition, a cultural tradition that was a part of the American mythology. It went along with George Washington and the cherry tree, and the Pilgrims and Thanksgiving. These were aspects of what it meant to be an American.

The postmodern generation grew up without a cultural allegiance to Christian ideas and values. It was not part of their frame of reference. They had not been exposed to it. They do not know the Christian concept of God or salvation. They are uninformed. They do not have a reason for regarding sex outside of marriage as wrong. Where would they be exposed to such an idea? They do not have a reason for questioning abortion as a civil right. There is no place that kind of view would be taught apart from a biblical context. They do not have a basis for examining the issue of euthanasia, which is the next major moral issue that is coming along. In all of these matters, no cultural norm exists for them because religion ceased to be an aspect of the culture in 1963. Therefore, they are thrown back on the only reliable authority they have: "Everyone did what seemed right in his own eyes," as we find in the book of Judges. They have no other basis.

It is interesting to note how this pluralistic system developed from 1963. Both political conservatives and political liberals advanced the pluralistic or valueless society from the 1960s on. Most people are familiar with the counterculture, which was an experiential approach to values. We think of the counterculture in terms of drugs, sex, and abandonment of norms of behavior. We also think of them in terms of experimentation with Eastern religions.

Not as much, though, do we think of the conservative libertarians. I became acquainted with them in the early 1970s. I had been politically active in the South and had assumed that to be politically conservative meant one was a Christian as well. It was that old Christendom idea. In 1970 I took part in the Institute on Comparative Political and Economic Systems at Georgetown University and held an internship in Congress for the summer. I found that most of the other participants in the program from other parts of the country who were politically conservative did not have faith. They advocated extreme individual freedom such that their behavior in terms of sex and drugs was exactly what I had experienced in college with people who were on the political left. In terms of morality, liberals and conservatives had similar behavior but for different reasons: one more experiential, the other more philosophical and intellectual, concerned with the advancement of laissez-faire, absolute freedom in personal decisions. Whereas the counterculture dominated the popular culture, the libertarian conservatives were active in the political structure that came to power in 1980 in Washington, D.C. Many of those people that had been involved in the program with me in 1970 were now involved in the Reagan administration and were carrying out a morally valueless political conservatism.

Now there has been a major shift in how cultural values are passed on. The institutions for passing on the cultural values have changed. In the old era, the church, the home, the school, and one's elders had the responsibility for passing on the values of the culture. In the present age, movies, television, music, and one's peers are responsible for the establishment of the cultural values. A media culture responds to the thoughts and desires of the youth generation.

In my first course in seminary in 1975, I read an article by Margaret Mead in an edited collection on anthropological subjects. I have searched in vain for that article many times since. In the article, which she would have written in the early 1960s or late 1950s, she predicted that we were entering a time in which no longer would the elder generation teach the younger generation, but that there would be a major cultural shift and the younger generation would determine the culture and teach it to the older generation. We have now arrived at that point. You can think in terms of how children teach their parents how to program the VCR.

WHAT'S THE MISSION?

One of the greatest difficulties Christians face in dealing with the challenge of pluralism involves understanding the primary Christian mission in the world. People have the dangerous tendency to run to polar extremes and miss the point. Some engage the world in a political battle to ensure the maintenance of a Christian society. Others withdraw from the world completely and abandon it to its own wickedness. The Amish withdrew from the world. The Puritans tried to take over the world. The Great Commission suggests another alternative in which the mission is to make disciples of Christ, and the methodology is through going about one's business in the world.

Both liberal and conservative Christians have attempted to resolve social problems through political activism in the twentieth century. Prohibition came about largely as a result of political pressure that sought a legal solution to the problem of alcohol abuse. In the 1950s and 1960s the cause of civil rights was advanced largely by activist Christians who helped ensure passage of the Voting Rights Act and the Civil Rights Act under the Johnson administration. In the late 1970s a burst of activism on the part of Christians sought to overturn the Supreme Court ruling that had the effect of legalizing abortion. Both liberals and conservatives opted for a political solution to problems in society, which conflicted with their understanding of the gospel.

Whatever else pluralism may mean, it certainly means the presence in society of multiple views and behaviors that conflict with the gospel. Throughout the twentieth century, Christians dealt with the emerging pluralism of the United States the way it had been treated traditionally during the long tenure of Christendom. Political power came into play to deal with views or behaviors that stood contrary to the current prevailing Christian consensus. For this approach to work, however, one needs a political majority. Nathan Bedford Forrest's famous strategy for victory also applies to politics: get there first with the most. Committed Christians constitute a minority of the American public today, and this minority includes Catholic, mainline Protestant, Evangelical, Charismatic/Pentecostal, and Orthodox Christians who do not always share a consensus understanding of Christian doctrine or behavior. In Western Europe, committed Christians represent a barely perceptible segment of the population. In terms of numbers, Christians cannot win a political struggle.

Tragically, for too many centuries Christians have sought political ways to enforce Christian discipleship upon people who do not follow Christ. We have sought to enforce godly behavior from ungodly people; thus, denying the very doctrines of salvation needed to make people godly. By the confusion of the Christian mission, we have tended to seek political solutions to spiritual problems while often ignoring social problems for which political solutions might have been found. The confusion of church and state has blurred the distinction between moral issues and religious issues. Moral issues transcend specific religious groups and even apply to nonreligious groups.

Most moral issues are endorsed by religious groups, but that endorsement does not make the issue a religious matter. For instance, most religious groups teach that it is wrong to steal. Similarly, a common teaching of religious groups relates to murder. The presence of common themes like these related to human behavior leads some people to conclude that all religions are basically the same. This view fails to appreciate that religion deals with a great deal more than morality. Despite many basic universal themes of morality, different religions inform and provide a foundation for those themes in different ways.

Many committed Christians in the United States feel the obligation that this country should operate according to the laws of God. In support of this view, many Old Testament texts about God's expectations for Israel may be found. This view tends to confuse the distinction between the old covenant between God and the particular nation of Israel, and the new covenant between God and his church. The first covenant established a nation, but the second transcends all cultures. As part of a democracy, Christians in the United States have a responsibility to influence the political processes as engaged citizens. On the other hand, we dare not suppose that the engines of politics and government can ever make society godly.

Conservative Christians who opposed the Civil Rights movement in the 1960s criticized their liberal brothers and sisters in the movement by declaring, "You can't legislate morality." By the late 1970s, however, conservative Christians had formed the Moral Majority to legislate morality. Because of the tendency to confuse religion and morality by both believers and non-believers alike, however, it appeared that Christians wanted to legislate religion.

Abortion is a moral issue related to life and death. In the cultural ferment of the 1970s it took on a different look. For the counterculture, abortion represented a civil right belonging to a woman. In the American tradition of the rugged individual and the conservative tradition of restricting governmental intrusion into the private lives of citizens, abortion became a privacy issue. Instead of dealing with abortion as a morality issue, however, conservative Christians tended to deal with it as a religious issue. While the Bible provides the basis for a Christian not to practice or endorse abortion, the rhetorical campaign that conservatives used had the effect of making it sound as though abortion was just a peculiar belief of a radical sect of religious people.

At this point, I am aware of several concerns. First, I want people to believe the Bible, place their faith in Christ through it, and rely upon it for guidance in the difficult issues of life. Second, I want the practice of random abortion on demand to die out. In a pluralistic culture I can endanger both of my concerns by an over-zealous attempt to force either to happen.

Fredericka Matthews-Greene and others like her have actually changed their strategy in the face of the dominance of pluralism in society today. From the old confrontational style of the 1960s, she has now embraced a style that lowers the temperature on the rhetoric and seeks to change people rather than defeat them.[1] One might call this approach "Christlike."

Abortion is not a religious issue, in the strict sense, but a moral issue. As such, it is not a church/state issue or even a matter of privacy, but a public policy issue over the civil rights of the unborn. In the famous Dred Scott case before the Civil War, the Supreme Court refused to decide in favor of the position of the slave Dred Scott because he was the legal property of another person. He was a slave, and therefore he had no rights. At the present moment, the Supreme Court has created the same situation for unborn children. Christians will have strong feelings about this matter, but it is not a religious issue and should not be confused as such.

Prayer in public schools, on the other hand, is a religious issue. Prayer is not a matter of morality but an exercise of religion. As such, it is a church/state issue and a matter of private choice. The right to pray is a civil right, but the governmental establishment of prayer is a public policy that violates the U.S. Constitution.

During the last half of the twentieth century, Christians in the United States have fallen into three camps related to the culture. Some have chosen to fight to maintain the culture as a vestige of Christian thought, value, and practice. These have sought to accomplish this aim through the use of politics. Some have ignored the rapidly changing culture and have even become a part of the valueless value system. Finally, a small group has sought to engage this culture like any other pagan culture that is hostile to Jesus Christ.

Christians who think their mission is to maintain control of society will suffer many bitter defeats in the days ahead. On the other hand, those who recognize that the United States now represents a great mission field and that we are aliens in it will find the next century filled with all the adventure of the first three centuries of the church.

RELIGIOUS PLURALISM

As early as 1975 the process theologian John Cobb expressed the logical implications of a long simmering trend in mainline Protestant circles. Pluralism had a modest beginning within the American church. It started small, but grew over the issue Christ raised at Caesarea Philippi: "Who do you say I am?" (Matt. 16:15).

John Cobb described several alternative approaches to pluralism within the church in *Christ in a Pluralistic Age*.[2] The approaches vary from a rejection of the claims of other religions to a rejection of the claims of Christianity. First, other religious ways have been seen as evil or false. Second, other religious ways have been described as anticipating Christ. Third, as Christians have come increasingly into contact with people of other religions, many have identified Christianity and other religions as the same reality. For instance, they may assert that Christ and Buddha are two names for the same reality. Fourth, when faced with the reality that Buddha and Christ actually stand for entirely different ideas of what is supremely important, many Christians opt for total relativism. This view would hold that all beliefs are culturally captive. This kind of relativism, however, results in a situation in which each religion has equal standing, but in which they are also closed, exclusive of each other, and limited. Fifth, Christians who want to be open to other religions may drop the terminology and image of Christ, resorting to vague terms such as "the ultimate" or "the divine spirit."

By 1987 Cobb's pluralism would seem tame compared with that of John

Hick, Paul Knitter, and a group of like-minded theologians who contributed to *The Myth of Christian Uniqueness: Toward a Pluralistic Theology of Religions*.[3] The pluralism of this volume expresses the pluralism of post-modernity and involves "a move away from insistence on the superiority or finality of Christ and Christianity toward a recognition of the independent validity of other ways." The new pluralism sees nothing unique about Christianity that sets it apart or above any other religion. In order to arrive at this final expression of the new pluralism, however, it was first necessary for Hick to settle the question Jesus asked at Caesarea Philippi. John Hick answered it in his volume *The Myth of God Incarnate*. Once he had dispensed with the incarnation, what was left of Christianity did not matter.[4]

If Christians are ambivalent, embarrassed, or hostile to the identity of Jesus as Christ, then one should not be surprised if society in general pays no attention to him. If Christians lose sight of Christ, then Christianity has nothing to offer. Apart from the incarnation of God in Jesus, Christianity has nothing unique to offer.

Pluralism did not arise as an attack from other religions. It did not come about as the result of Supreme Court decisions or hostile politicians. Pluralism within society poses nothing but opportunity for the gospel, but pluralism within the Christian community arises because Christians have abandoned their Lord in exchange for religion.

The apostles found the pluralism of the Roman Empire fertile soil in which to plant the gospel. In a sense, the apostles had an easier job of dealing with the pluralism of the empire because they knew they had to win a hearing. Christians who have a strong sense of the traditional place of Christianity within Western society may feel a degree of resentment when the public does not give Christianity its traditional role.

Freed from its traditional role, however, Christianity returns to its primitive vitality. Losing all advantage and privilege in society, Christianity no longer has anything about it to hold the allegiance of people, unless they can answer the question of Jesus the way Peter did. The danger for committed Christians during this time of dramatic and far-reaching cultural change is that they will be more concerned about the standing of the Christian religion in society than about the standing of Jesus Christ within his church.

INTOLERANCE?

In one sense, Jesus Christ represents the kind of pluralism that accepts all people and makes of them one family. A certain kind of pluralism existed in the days of the Roman Empire, which allowed for great diversity of religious expression, as long as ultimate loyalty was paid to Rome. This pluralism, however, had no intention of making one great Roman family of all the peoples of the empire. All the peoples shared the privilege of subjugation by Rome. Very few people held citizenship with all the rights, privileges, and responsibilities appertaining thereto. The pluralism of Rome represented a carefully defined toleration of differences. The toleration worked when no one had rights.

A similar kind of toleration occurred within the police states of totalitarian Communism. The Communist bloc included wildly diverse groups that could be divided ethnically, linguistically, racially, and religiously. Marshall Tito governed a unified Yugoslavia that appeared to be a model of tolerance between groups within a pluralistic society. With Tito's death and the collapse of the Communist system, Yugoslavia split apart into warring factions. Ancient differences and hatreds that go back to the days of the Byzantine Empire surfaced as soon as the restraints disappeared.

The *Pax Romana* was just the sort of peace as that enforced by totalitarian government. People got along at the point of a sword. By and large, people do not get along. The pluralism of postmodernity confines itself largely to English-speaking North America and a few countries of Western Europe. For the most part, the pluralism of the postmodern age is a phenomenon of the affluent West. If anything, ethnicity and tribalism are on the rise. The hatred and killing in Northern Ireland struggles with an uneasy and fragile truce. The Bosnians, Serbs, and Croats of former Yugoslavia have fought a series of wars with each other over the last ten years with no reason to believe that another war might not break out. More than fifty years after the bloody division of the old British colony of India, predominantly Muslim Pakistan and predominantly Hindu India continue to threaten war with each other. Inside India strife continues between Sikhs, Hindus, and Muslims. In the former Soviet Union war broke out between Armenia and Azerbaijan. In Sudan the Arabic government of the north has fought for years against black African insurgents in the south. The Middle East has witnessed fifty years of strife between Jews and Arabs. Each of these episodes involves a religious dimension.

The religions of the world are mutually exclusive. The intensity of feeling generated by religious conflict bears testimony to this fact. Even those religions that claim to make room for all the other religions do so only on their terms. In this sense, Christianity is no different from any other religion in making truth claims. Each religion, in making its own claims, declares the other religions to be false. Christianity is no different from any other religion in this regard. The difference for Christianity lies in the fact that the current experiment with pluralism is taking place in territory once regarded as a Christian land. Several areas of confusion have clouded the issues involved for people.

Pluralism cannot exist in human society without the force of law. Pluralism does not require totalitarian dictatorship, but it does require the consistent administration of the law. In ancient Rome and the modern communist state, everyone shared equal oppression. In American and British democracy, people share equal rights and protection under the law. It is one theory to say that Christians may not legislate their religious beliefs and impose them on a nonbelieving citizenry. It is quite another to say that Christians may not exercise their right to practice their religion.

Unfortunately, Christianity relied upon its position within the prevailing culture rather than on the proclamation of the gospel to ensure its survival. Survival and maintenance of the status quo are not very lofty goals. The primary function of the Christian faith is to proclaim the gospel to those who do not have faith in Jesus Christ. Proclamation from a position of power can confuse the one proclaiming and the one hearing. A certain satisfaction comes in declaring the truth as we know it, as Jonah did. We can forget that we do not proclaim the gospel for our satisfaction, but so that someone else can come to know Christ in such a way that they have faith in him.

In the postmodern age, Christianity has lost its position of cultural power. It has not disappeared by any means, and it continues to have many great institutions at its disposal as well as millions of adherents. Yet, it has lost its position of power within the culture. Christians must now ask, "How do we proclaim the gospel from a position of weakness?" Fortunately, we have centuries of experience doing just that.

The gospel always calls for confrontation. Yet, we sometimes forget who is doing the confronting. The confrontation comes between Jesus Christ and the people we tell about him. The confrontation should never be between us and the ones we tell. The proclamation from a position of privilege and power tends to foster personal conflict rather than divine confrontation. The gospel always carries a threat because it claims our very lives; therefore, the threat of the gospel needs to come from Christ, not from Christians.

Deprived of the position of power, however, Christians may once again begin to experience the only power that matters. In a state of cultural powerlessness, people become free to experience the power Christ promised. When Patrick journeyed to Ireland fifteen hundred years ago, he left the security of Christendom to enter the land of Celtic paganism. He entered a land of egregarious pagan worship practices. As often as not, they sacrificed their own babies to the Druid gods. Within a generation, however, the Emerald Isle had become a Christian land. Patrick spoke from a position of weakness, but he did so with the power of God. In the face of pluralism, it helps to recall that the power of God is stronger than the power of cultural convention.

The attitude of Christians will determine their effectiveness in the new pluralistic culture. In the last years of cultural dominance, Christians were strangely silent within the broad culture as they seemed content to let Billy Graham fulfill the Great Commission vicariously for all believers. Christians with a willingness to let their faith out of the box will have opportunities in a pluralistic age to talk about the significance of Jesus Christ. The greatest opportunities will come in the marketplace of day-to-day life. In the twentieth century, personal witnessing tended to mean the delivery of a lecture prescribed by a tract or a model presentation. In a pluralistic age, the Christian who can speak specifically of Christ to an individual will demonstrate why Christ stands out from the many alternatives. Conversation replaces the lecture for the Christian who demonstrates the personal concern of Christ. The willingness to speak goes along with a willingness to listen to the concerns of people living in a hollow world.

Several models exist that show Christians how to make the most of the opportunities that arise as a result of the new pluralism. Pluralism had become the rule in the academic world long before it became the norm of Western culture. Long before the term *postmodernity* came into usage, C. S. Lewis had critiqued the drift he observed in academic culture. In *The Abolition of Man* and other writings, Lewis laid out the subtlety of the introduction of relativism into English school texts in Britain. Without going into Lewis's astute analysis of the relativizing trend in culture, we may learn a great deal about how he addressed the problem.

Lewis lived in a country that is a Christian nation by law. The Church of England is the official religion, and the monarch is head of the church. Furthermore, official prayers are said in all public schools, and religious instruction is required as part of the educational system. Despite this significant official support of Christianity, only 2 percent of the population attend church on any regular basis. Lewis did not seek more legislation to protect the position of Christianity, nor did he seek to elect politicians who could turn the country around spiritually. Politicians and courts respond to the culture. They do not change the culture.

Lewis went to work in his little corner of the culture. Lewis became, perhaps, the most significant witness to Christ in the English-speaking world in the twentieth century. Unlike professionally religious people like Billy Graham, Martin Luther King, Jr., Mother Teresa, and Albert Schweitzer, Lewis earned his living as an English teacher and had no official role in the church. He merely lived out his faith in the place where he happened to work, Oxford University. Lewis serves as a model for how a Christian can have an impact in a pluralistic culture. Literally thousands of people have become Christians because of him, and hundreds of thousands have probably changed the way they think about the world because of him. Most of Oxford did not agree with Lewis at the time, but they had to take him seriously. By its very nature, a pluralistic culture is one in which all ideas stand shoulder to shoulder, but someone must be willing to express the ideas. Lewis gained a hearing for several reasons.

First, Lewis worked hard and did good work. He had the professional respect of those who knew him. He made his mark as a first-rate scholar of Medieval and Renaissance English literature, contributing several important volumes to the field. More than this, however, he understood his first priority belonged to his students. He worked hard as a teacher, and his students proved it.

Second, Lewis claimed no special privilege as the one who brought the gospel. For those who believe the gospel, it is the power of God unto salvation; but for those who do not yet know the gospel, it is folly (Rom. 1:16, 1 Cor. 1:18). Not until a person believes in Christ can he or she realize the privileged position of everyone who knows Christ. That privileged position, however, relates to our standing with God. As such, Lewis presented the gospel as new information to many people. He presented it to educated people as Paul presented it to the Athenians. He recognized their ignorance of spiritual matters and explained Christianity one step at a time. He made no assumptions about what his audience ought to know, how they ought to think, how they ought to behave. A person who does not know Christ does not yet have the option of living in a way Christ approves.

Third, Lewis was willing to do the appropriate thing in the circumstances. He never bullied his students into becoming Christians. One passionate atheist avoided tutorials with "the mad dog Christian" because he had the impression that Lewis would be a "pale and cadaverous moralist" who would try to draw some "trite Christian moralization from every text." He eventually changed his mind because he so resented not being able to study medieval English literature because of Lewis. In three years of meeting together for weekly tutorials, Lewis never once raised the issue of faith. Instead of a preachy clergyman, Lewis turned out to be a robust man full of life. The tutorial always focused on the opinions of the young student whom Lewis treated with courtesy as a "junior colleague." When the young man finished his time at Oxford, he now resented being deprived of the person who meant the most to him.[5] Lewis always respected people. On the other hand, he was not shy about expressing himself. He could go from the private tutorial with a student to the public lecture hall where he would hammer away at the criticism of faith. He understood this difference between stating an opinion and giving the reason for an opinion. Peter enjoins us to always be prepared to give a *reason* for the hope we have (1 Pet. 3:15). He loved a good, public debate, but he also understood when to listen. He knew the difference between winning an argument and winning a convert.

Fourth, Lewis was good company. He cultivated the art of conversation, which involves the obligation not to bore. Being good company requires that a person genuinely be interested in others. In a pluralistic society, the legitimacy of any idea, religion, or belief will often depend upon the character and personal qualities of the person expressing them. For Lewis, this quality expressed itself in many forms of consideration, but perhaps none more important than his constant willingness to take time for family, friends, colleagues, students, and total strangers.

The C. S. Lewis Foundation has taken Lewis as its model to encourage Christian professors in secular institutions to be Christians like Lewis. In the marketplace of ideas, the Christian perspective has as much place as any other idea. In the marketplace of ideas, the gospel can hold its own. The only question concerns whether anyone will be willing to express it.

CHAPTER THREE

GET YOUR ACT TOGETHER: WHOLENESS

In the movie *Bridge Over the River Kwai*, a British colonel in a prisoner of war camp becomes totally preoccupied with his task of building a bridge across a river. He builds a magnificent bridge—a bridge that he hopes will last for hundreds of years and that the people will remember. He is focused on this small task. In the midst of the task, however, he loses the big picture and does not realize the effect of building this bridge. The bridge he built is used for the Japanese army to carry troops in order to fight the British. He becomes a traitor to his own cause because he is so preoccupied with one task that he cannot see the effect of his action on others.

This approach to life is typical of the modern world. The modern world divided everything up into specializations so that life became fragmented and disconnected. People lost a sense of the whole—of how everything related to everything else. We see this fragmentation in all levels of society. We experience it with the government, which we ridicule as the bureaucracy. Who has not had the experience of going first to one office and then another where they shuffle you around and pass the buck? You never get an answer because each office is dealing with one little specialization, and they tell us, "Well, I don't do that."

A similar thing has happened in medicine. When I was a little boy people had a family doctor, but as time passed everything became a specialization. Now we have doctors for skin and doctors for backs and doctors for just about everything. Now I go to an internist. An internist cannot, so far as I can tell, really help you; but at least he knows which of his friends probably can. Everything's a specialization. The joke in education is that a Ph.D. is somebody who knows more and more about less and less. Dissertation titles reflect this pursuit of narrow expertise. My dissertation has the embarrassingly narrow title of *Evangelistic Fervency Among the Puritans in Stuart England, 1603–1688*. Even in high school students begin to experience the fragmentation of knowledge and experience. They study many subjects, but rarely do the subjects connect. They study English over here, and math over here, and history somewhere else; but students are left wondering, "What does this have to do with life?" Where does it come together? The standard answer to this question from my seminary professors was, "Well, I just give you the theory—I let you work it out." Great!

After school, the average American experiences fragmentation in the work place. The assembly line is perhaps one of the greatest representations of specialization, where people can spend thirty years just tightening one screw, and that's all they do. They specialize in that one piece, but they never have the opportunity of putting together the whole thing. No one has the sense of pride and accomplishment that comes from actually building the washing machine or the car. This is what sets Rolls Royce apart from all other cars, because a team gets together and builds a whole car. Each Rolls is a masterpiece of these people working together on the whole thing. They form a team, and they take pride in what they do.

The church in the United States, unfortunately, adopted the worldview of the modern age. We adopted the methodology, and we bought into the idea of specialization. I have spent my life as a Southern Baptist. The Southern Baptist Convention represents modernity at its most efficient. The Baptist Program could be found in virtually every Southern Baptist church. Southern Baptist churches had graded Sunday school from the cradle to the grave. They had graded choirs from preschool through adults. They had graded missions organizations for men and for women. They had a graded program of discipleship training separate from Sunday school. The Baptist Program represented all the different specializations of church life, but rarely did the pieces ever come together. For all of the activity, each church might have been running five or six entirely different, independent church programs. That fragmentation characterizes the modern age. Every denomination had its counterpart to the Southern Baptist Program.

The Baptist Program worked very well, and provided Southern Baptists with a structure that propelled them to unparalleled growth among American denominations. That experience represents another thing about the modern age. We concentrated on what works. But a lot of people, the postmodern people, have voted "no." They voted no because they no longer come. They do not participate. The assembly-line approach to faith no longer meets their spiritual needs, so they stay home. The specialization mentality characterized the conflict between different divisions or agencies of the different denominations. There was tremendous turf fighting between agencies over who was in charge of important or popular ministries. Jealousy and power politics ensued if one agency started doing what the other one perceived as their area of specialization. This way of relating is typical of the modern age.

Now, the postmodern generation has cried out for things to be pooled together. They live lives strung apart. Their lives are hectic. The lives of the older, modern generation are hectic, too—but we came into it from an easier time, just like the frog in the pot of water, who, when the heat is turned on gradually, will stay there until it is cooked. Modern Christians have been in church from the time it was simple, and they have grown up cooked. The modern generation stayed with it. The difference with the postmodern generation is that they do not have the loyalty. They will not stick with it, because they do not like all the different pieces. They do not want to be pulled in different directions in their personal life. They want to see how all the pieces fit together.

Christians who have been around for a long time absorbed how one area of church life relates to the rest of the church, and how discipleship training prepares church leaders by giving them an understanding of doctrine, methodology, missions, and polity. The postmodern generation has no reason to understand or appreciate any of the denominational program. They do not like the conflict of competing specializations and departments, and they do not like turf warfare. For them, church often looks like just another organization, and they do not want to belong to an organization that adds another specialization to their lives.

DEPTH OF FRAGMENTATION

Modernity destroyed something about the human possibility of even understanding how the varied pieces of life fit together. In an agrarian culture, people understood the relationships of life. They did not necessarily understand the relationships as a result of thinking about it. They experienced the process. Over time they knew that having wheat for bread meant plowing, disking, sowing, cultivating, and harvesting. Having clothes to wear involved these processes for cotton and flax, plus another set of related experiences in caring for animals that finally resulted in wool. With the raw cotton, wool, or flax, a person could then begin yet another set of related experiences involving cleaning, dying, carding, spinning, and weaving. Modern urban people only see the finished product. Modern people depend upon instant satisfaction. We have lost the sense of time, work, and relationship involved in the ordinary processes of life.

During the earlier part of the twentieth century, an expression arose to indicate the significance of something. If it was truly grand, it was said to be "the greatest thing since sliced bread." Modernity praised the separation of people from the basic process of life. At the end of the twentieth century, one of the growing fads of urban dwellers involved the making of homemade bread. People did not grow the wheat, but they combined all the ingredients themselves and took the time to bake the bread. A Vietnam veteran told me that he bakes bread every Saturday and regards it as a mystical experience that involves the essence of life. One might say that it functioned as a sacrament for him.

The postmodern people feel that something is missing, but they are not sure what. Note that they *feel* something is missing. They did not arrive at this view necessarily from thought. When our bodies do not feel right, we go to a doctor to find out what is wrong. Feelings give us information, but they do not tell the whole story. Part of the tragedy of the fragmentation of modernity involves the separation of thought and emotion. Both are important, but neither by itself tells the whole story.

The modern world blossomed in an atmosphere that exalted reason and ridiculed emotion. Such terms as "the Enlightenment" and "the Age of Reason" described the dawning of the modern age. This attitude toward reason set heart and mind against each other. This fragmentation appears most graphically in the career of that most excellent literary character, Sherlock Holmes. In explaining why he had no room for love and romance in his life, Holmes explained to his friend Watson, "But love is an emotional thing, and whatever is emotional is opposed to that true cold reason which I place above all things. I should never marry myself, lest I bias my judgment."[1]

Sherlock Holmes went further in his fragmentation. Not only did he not want to deal with the emotional dimension of life, he wanted only the kind of rational knowledge that pertained to his work. For Holmes, knowledge was utilitarian and pragmatic. He further explained to Watson:

> I consider that a man's brain originally is like a little empty attic, and you have to stock it with such furniture as you choose. A fool takes in all the lumber of every sort that he comes across, so that the knowledge which might be useful to him gets crowded out, or at least is jumbled up with a lot of other things, so that he has difficulty in laying his hands upon it.[2]

The specialist Holmes describes seems not unreasonable, especially when he devotes himself to ridding London of the basest criminals. Of course, most fragmented modernists are not Sherlock Holmes. They do not spend their mental energies outwitting the criminal element. Instead, they know all about their job, which bores them and everyone else.

In this state of boredom, the postmodern generation has turned to Thomas Jefferson's ideal: the pursuit of happiness. As a child of the Enlightenment, however, Jefferson represents fragmentation at its most colorful. The fundamental flow in his rhetoric is the notion that happiness can be pursued. It suggests that a person can find happiness outside themselves. My Constitutional History professor in college taught that Jefferson meant "property" when he spoke of the pursuit of happiness. Either way the flow remains. People have the notion that happiness or the missing ingredient of life lies outside them in either some activity or some object. They are in pursuit of the secular sacrament.

In recent years as the postmodern generation has grown increasingly aware that something is missing, a variety of approaches or techniques have arisen to satisfy the feeling. Within the field of counseling and therapy, in particular, several terms have emerged. One approach was to "get in touch with your feelings." This approach acknowledges the modern tendency to deaden the emotions and the ability to deal with emotions. Another approach would have us "get in touch with the child within." This approach suggests that something was lost a long time ago and that somehow it can be reclaimed from childhood. This approach reflects the yearning for something lost or missing, like Citizen Kane whispering "Rosebud."

Unfortunately, these cures are as much a part of the problem as fragmentation. Fragmentation is just one of the many plagues of modernity. Reductionism is another. Reductionism reduces an explanation to just one cause. Thus, if we get in touch with the child within, we solve the problem. If we get in touch with our feelings, we solve the problem. Part of the problem with ever finding a way out of the fragmentation rests in the reductionist assumption. Life is more complicated than that. Like baking bread or making a shirt, life can bog down at any one of many different steps along the way.

Why do some people feel torn apart in a life situation in which someone else seems to function fine? Part of the answer lies in the extent to which people are "whole" or complete. Since Charles Darwin, the modern world has tended to view people as purely physical in nature with a collection of assorted body parts that serve different functions. In this view, reason and emotion are nothing more than chemical reactions. "Bad" emotions and thoughts arise as a result of a chemical imbalance. The logical fallacy arises from concluding that all of emotion and thought can be explained as a chemical reaction because a chemical imbalance in the body affects emotion and reason.

As postmodern people have grown increasingly aware of the failure of reductionism in general and of naturalism in particular, they have grown aware of the spiritual dimension of people. Eastern religions offer a perspective on wholeness that liberal Christianity had cast aside. At a seminar on science and faith in Toronto sponsored by the John Templeton Foundation, I met a sociologist from Canada who was studying the approach of a Hindu doctor to holistic medicine. When I asked her if she had explored any of the Christian tradition of healing, she said that she did not know much about Christianity. She had not rejected the traditional religion of her culture. She simply did not know about it.

Deeply embodied in the biblical understanding of people lies the understanding of the unity of body and spirit, even though the two are quite different. A body without a spirit is a corpse, and a spirit without a body is a ghost. Neither is fully itself apart from the dynamic relationship that exists between the two. In Genesis 2, we find a graphic picture of this relationship as God breathes into a clay statue and it becomes a "breathing being" or soul. People do not have a soul; they are a soul. In the language of Zion, when God saves our soul, he saves all of us. The idea of resurrection that lies at the heart of the Christian faith emphasizes this totality of body and spirit as the human soul.

The Greeks had an entirely different concept of body and soul. They believed that the soul was eternal, that it existed prior to being imprisoned in a body, and that it would escape to the spiritual realm once the body died. They viewed the soul as good and the body as bad. This concept of the two as opposed to one another is referred to as dualism. Hebrew thought insisted that the physical and spiritual dimensions of a person exist as a unity and that they were originally conceived and created by God as good. Just as sin destroys a person's relationship with God, it also destroys the unity of body and spirit. The appropriate relationship fragments. The apostle Paul described this breakdown in Galatians where he spoke of it as a war between the flesh and the spirit.

While Eastern religions aim at wholeness or completion, they do so in a different way than Christianity. While Hinduism advocates an essential unity, it achieves this unity by denying the true reality of the particulars. In Hindu thought, all is one. A body is an aspect of everything, not just of one particular person. In fact, no one actually exists as a particular person. Only the unity is real. Buddhism also advocates a unity of all things, but it denies the true reality of the physical. The illusion of the physical world creates the experience of fragmentation for the soul, which has not lost itself in the unconscious unity of all reality. In contrast to these views, the Hebrew understanding of the person regards the physical body as a real and human personality, unique and distinct from God and other people.

THE BODY/SPIRIT UNITY

The Hebrew scriptures describe people as souls composed of a personal, unique spirit that is intimately, uniquely, and inseparably related to a real physical body. Modern scientific naturalism denies the spirit while Eastern monism denies the body and particularity of individual people.

The apostle Paul spoke at length on this fundamental understanding and its relationship to everyday life. Fragmentation has occurred in some way in every society that provides for any kind of social structure. Paul used the metaphor of the body to describe human corporate relationships within the church and the relationship of individuals to Christ. People relate to themselves in their uniqueness and difference from other people like the organs or "members" of a body.

This metaphor represents an objective view of the universe and the existence of particular things. It assumes that at a basic level we can have some confidence that our sense of perception can be relied upon for a practical knowledge of the world. In contrast to monism, which views everything as actually one thing, this view believes in distinctions between things. The eyes really exist, and they do something different from the ears or the lungs.

At the same time, the example of the body demonstrates the interdependent nature of reality. This view represents a relational model rather than a naturalistic cause-and-effect model. If I injure my foot, the pain is not felt merely in my foot. It may be localized there, but the whole of me experiences pain. It affects my ability to think about other things. If my kidney begins to malfunction, it affects my whole body. Illness tends to always be localized, yet it affects the whole body. I can lose some body parts without dying, yet the whole of me is diminished. I can lose other body parts and all of me will die. The parts are real, unique, and functionally different, yet belong to a larger whole. The Christian faith affirms both the value of the individual and corporate responsibility and belonging. The fragmentation of modernity has continually forced the false issue that would press Christians to opt for one or the other of these modes of expression.

Before leaving the metaphor of the body and its members to explore the relationship between body and spirit, we can see that this basic understanding of human nature has an application to social relationships. The Bible assumes the unity in diversity of the human body. This same unity in diversity applies to the ideal social relationship known as the church, or the Body of Christ.

Just as a human body with ailing parts results in a sick person, a social relationship's health depends upon the completeness of those who make up the relationship. It only takes one incomplete person to make an ailing social group. The old saying "One rotten apple spoils the lot" refers to this condition.

Just as a lung cannot really be a healthy lung apart from its relationship to the rest of the human body, a Christian cannot really be a growing, vital Christian apart from his or her relationship to the other members of the Body of Christ. The problem of fragmentation of social relationships goes back to the beginning of human experience, and Christ offers a solution to the problem of fragmented relationships in society based on relationship to him.

As the opening of Genesis paints a picture of human nature, God declares that it is not good for people to be alone. People are meant for relationship, yet human history is the sad story of the failure of human relationships. In praying for his disciples, however, Jesus presented the model for wholeness in human relationship. He prayed for human unity based on relationship to him rooted in the unity of the Father and the Son. In the Father and the Son we see the intrinsic relationship between spirit and body modeled. Though the Father and the Son are real, separate persons, they belong to each other as one God.

Returning to the model of the human body, we see that the physical unity has diverse and unique parts. The biblical understanding of the human spirit has an equal complexity. It does not do simply to reduce the conflict of the human spirit to the difference between heart and mind. In the Hebrew understanding of people, the mind belongs to the heart! In the Psalms and throughout the Old Testament the heart serves as a poetic metaphor for the human spirit.

When King David sang, "Create in me a clean heart, O God; and renew a right spirit within me" (Ps. 51:10 KJV), he was not referring to two things: heart and spirit. Instead of rhyming, Hebrew poetry makes its mark by saying one thing in two ways. The Hebrew correlation of the human spirit with a physical part of the body, however, suggests the strong relationship between body and spirit.

A number of biblical references point up the fact that a weakened body diminishes the spirit and a weakened spirit diminishes the body. When Jacob *heard* the news that Joseph his beloved son was still alive, and *saw* the wagons loaded with food that Joseph had sent, his spirit revived (Gen. 45:27). News that the Jordan River had dried up to allow the Israelites to enter the promised land caused the Canaanite kings to lose heart (Josh. 5:1). The spirit of Samson revived when he drank (Judg. 15:19). The spirit of an Egyptian slave revived when he ate (1 Sam. 30:12). The spirit of the Queen of Sheba faded when she saw that Solomon could answer all of her questions (1 Kings 10:5, 2 Chron. 9:4). A Hebrew proverb states this idea simply:

> A man's spirit sustains him in sickness,
>   but a crushed spirit who can bear? (Prov. 18:14)

When the disciples could not stay awake to watch for him while he prayed on the night he was arrested, Jesus observed, "The spirit is willing, but the body is weak" (Matt. 26:41). In other words, the weakness (tiredness) of the body affected the exercise of the will.

How multidimensional is the human spirit that can so easily feel torn and fragmented? It is probably not possible to give an absolute answer. An examination of the kinds of words that describe the human spirit in the Bible provides a basis for grouping dimensions of the spirit into broad categories. This method may seem frustrating because categories tend to overlap, which is precisely the point. One dimension of the spirit has an impact on another. The modern desire to have neat, discrete categories does not correspond to the mess of the human spirit.

Some references suggest that the spirit represents the domain of the intellect and the will:

willing understanding	Exodus 35:21, Job 20:3
inquiry	Psalm 77:6
enlightenment	Proverbs 20:27
discernment	Proverbs 18:15
self-control	Proverbs 25:28

Some references suggest that the spirit represents the domain of vitality and life:

revive	Genesis 45:27
preserve	Job 10:12
breaks	Psalm 76:12
fails	Psalm 143:7
faint and melt	Ezekiel 21:7

Some references suggest that the spirit represents the domain of the emotions:

troubled	Genesis 41:8
anguished	Exodus 6:9 (KJV)
sullen	1 Kings 21:5
bitter	Ezekiel 3:14
distressed	Isaiah 54:6

Some references suggest that the spirit represents the domain of character and attitude:

obstinate	Deuteronomy 2:30
deceit	Psalm 32:2
unfaithful	Psalm 78:8
quick-tempered	Proverbs 14:29
haughty	Proverbs 16:18
humble	Proverbs 16:19
patient	Ecclesiastes 7:8
proud	Ecclesiastes 7:8
innocent	Proverbs 16:2
trustworthy	Proverbs 11:13

These lists represent just a brief selection of references to the human spirit. They are not presented in any organized, systematic way in the Bible. They merely appear in the stories about certain people who have encountered God.

I have made reference to these domains of the human spirit in other books. Here I speak of only four basic domains, but I have spoken of five and six. I have even drawn diagrams to illustrate how the discrete domains influence one another, but these are modern rather than postmodern attempts to describe scientifically something that cannot be known by the scientific method.[3] Rather than circles and lines, it may be more helpful to think of a big plate of spaghetti. All the different strands of spiritual existence are too tangled to say that intellect and character can be neatly isolated. Stubbornness affects one's ability to make reasonable decisions. Depression affects the exercise of the will. Pride can distort understanding. Poor discernment can create grief.

The sense of fragmentation within a person comes when we lose the equilibrium necessary to keep the fullness of the soul in balance. By ignoring one aspect of what it means to be human while indulging another aspect, the basis for unity loses its impact. This loss of equilibrium looks different in all people. Like Sherlock Holmes, we may indulge the intellect and ignore the capacity for love, which leaves a person emotionally immature. Like Casanova, we may indulge the physical sensations of sex and ignore the emotional capacity for intimacy and commitment, which leaves a person emotionally retarded. Like Falstaff, we may indulge the physical appetite for food and drink and ignore the character capacity for self-control, which leaves a person physically unhealthy. Literature has chronicled this universal problem of disequilibrium and refers to it as the "tragic flaw." An otherwise commendable person always has a fault, perhaps known only to the self or to a small few, which damages the person and his or her most important relationships.

The problem of fragmentation during modernity has seemed more intense than in the past perhaps because the normal constraints that a culture devises to protect us from ourselves and minimize the effects of fragmentation have all but disappeared. Society has destroyed most of the old restraints in the West. The entertainment industry has replaced school, church, and home as the primary institution for teaching and preserving values in society. For pure entertainment value, the focus of movies, television, and music recording tends toward a narrow range of dimensions of the soul. The themes relate to sex, violence, vanity, and pride. Such themes as self-control, patience, humility, and sacrifice rarely make it because they do not have the same entertainment value. In most cultures the institutions for teaching and preserving the values also serve to help people restrain the tendency toward disequilibrium. In the West, however, the new institution of entertainment exists to encourage overindulgence and abandonment of restraint. The entertainment industry exists to cater to the fantasies of the public.

Without wholeness at the personal level, societies quickly fall into disequilibrium. They tend to allow one or two dimensions of the soul to define them. The city-states of ancient Greece illustrate this tendency. The harsh, military outlook of Sparta has given us the term "spartan." Corinth was noted in ancient times for its sensuality and sexual overindulgence. Athens gained a reputation as an intellectual center. These differences inevitably led to the Peloponnesian War, which effectively destroyed the autonomous existence of the city-states involved. Left weakened and dissipated, they were easily conquered by the Macedonians.

In modern times, the growth of fragmentation in American society can be observed in the difference between how we conducted World War II and the Vietnam War. Whether at the personal level of the soul or the social level of a nation, people need some basis for integration. People tend to fragment. Society tends to fragment; therefore, some focus must serve as a basis for pulling the pieces together into a whole. In World War II, the Allies had a clear mission. Churchill and Roosevelt articulated more than slogans and propaganda. They clearly laid out the mission of the war, and in so doing they provided people with a sense of purpose that bound the people together. The Vietnam War did not have the same sense of mission and purpose. Instead of uniting the nation, the Vietnam War tore the nation apart. The presence or absence of a sense of mission and purpose had a profound impact on the course of the two wars.

In World War II, the presence of a clear, commonly held mission led to a grand and historic expression of strategy. Strategy represents the military concept of typing together all of the pieces on a grand scale. For instance, the Allied invasion of Normandy stands out as one of the greatest strategic initiatives in military history. It involved the largest armada ever assembled and included the navies of many nations. For it to work, however, all the pieces had to work together. The meteorologists had to identify the time when the weather would be best for the operation. The airborne divisions had to parachute behind enemy lines during the night and disrupt communications. The navies had to transport troops from England to France. The mine sweepers had to clear the mines so the troop ships could approach land. The combat engineers had to clear the mines on land for the advancing land troops. The quartermaster corps had to assemble sufficient supplies and transportation to sustain the operation. The signal corps had to establish communication links for the whole operation. The strategy required that all the pieces do what they were intended to do in the proportion in which they were intended to do it. Napoleon learned the hard way that it does no good to focus all one's energies on advancing with the finest troops if the supply lines are not maintained.

In Vietnam the absence of a clear, commonly held mission led to a war without strategy. The war involved all of the same components: Navy, Air Force, Army, Marines. The components included the same functions: combat, supplies, communications. In Vietnam, however, none of it had a purpose. The air force bombed Hanoi, but for no apparent reason other than a show of force. Troops were ordered to take a village, then go and take a crossroads, then go and take a bridge, then go and take a hill, and finally go and take the village again before starting all over. All the pieces were present. All the activity of war went on, but nothing had a purpose to hold it together and give it a direction. Nothing held the pieces in balance.

It only took one generation for the fragmentation to become complete. A sense of national purpose has disappeared. On the personal level individuals struggle with the issue of purpose, meaning, and identity. Without these matters resolved, it is virtually impossible to deal with the tornness that arises from living in a fragmented world. Without an integrating purpose, people have no basis for pulling the pieces together in their own soul or dealing with the many forces that would pull them apart.

PULLING THE PIECES TOGETHER AGAIN

In that context, what opportunity do Christians have for reaching the postmodern generation? The gospel brought the stinging critique to fragmentation long before the postmodern generation thought of it. The last night

Jesus was with his disciples, gathered together in the room, he said, "My peace I give unto you. Not as the world gives, give I thee." Jesus offers a basis for having wholeness in a fragmented world.

The postmodern generation's distaste for fragmentation and their longing for wholeness will not make the fragmentation of an increasingly complex society go away, nor will it lead to wholeness. Part of the charm of pluralism lies in the possibility that it can end the experience of fragmentation. Pluralism rejects the idea of differences in an effort to make people one. At the same time, it accepts all the differences by denying the differences. In order to do this, however, it requires that we disregard the aspect of people that makes critical judgments and assigns value. In this sense pluralism actually heightens the experience of fragmentation by ignoring the distinction between the equality of people and the equality of behavior. All people are acceptable, but not all behavior is acceptable. By denying moral judgment and its intrinsic relationship to the human spirit, we remove the restraints on individual behavior and the social fabric. By not allowing for moral judgment, people become alienated within themselves. The error of postmodern people has been to think that wholeness comes through the avoidance of conflict. Wholeness only shows itself in strength in the process of conflict. The conflict provides the heat that melds us together.

When Jesus spoke of peace, he used an ancient term. That ancient Hebrew word *Shalom*, which we translate peace, expresses the idea of "wholeness." A modern-day person might use a term like "Get your act together. Pull yourself together." It's the idea of having all the pieces back where they're supposed to be no matter what's coming at you. And Jesus says, "That's what I will do for you." The world's idea of peace is "We're not actually killing each other right now." This worldly approach to peace characterizes what peaceful coexistence was like with the Soviet Union back in the sixties when we were all building bomb shelters. We were not killing each other, but we were ready for war at any moment. That was "peace." Jesus says, "That's the way the world gives you peace." Worrying if somebody is going to break into your house or mug you represents an absence of peace. Maybe you have not been robbed, but the anxiety is there. Jesus says, "I'm not going to give you that kind of peace." In the midst of the conflict and the strife coming from every direction with all of the pieces of life pulling in a thousand directions, Jesus said "I'm going to give you peace. I will be your peace."

For the soul to have peace, all of the aspects of the spirit need to work together in harmony with one another and in relation to the body. Jesus Christ offers a relational solution to the dilemma. The fragmentation that people experience represents one dimension of the absence of a relationship with God. Fragmentation represents one of the aspects of the experience of sin in a person's life. The experience does not exhaust the meaning of sin, but on a day-to-day basis it provides the best gauge for realizing that something is out of balance in a relationship with God.

Peace for the soul begins with peace with God. Another way to think of fragmentation is alienation. The act of bringing together what has been alienated is called *reconciliation*. Accountants perform this act every day. They search columns of numbers to find why they are out of balance. One of the columns has an error and the error must be corrected. Accountants refer to the act of correcting the error and changing it to conform to the right figure as *reconciling* the error. Jesus Christ came into the world to reconcile us to God. People have fragmented lives, alienated from themselves and others, because they are out of balance with God. They are alienated from God and need to be reconciled to God.

In writing to the Romans, Paul explained that "we have peace with God through our Lord Jesus Christ" (Rom. 5:1) and that this peace works to bring wholeness to our life experiences. He observed that "we also rejoice in our sufferings, because we know that suffering produces perseverance; perseverance, character; and character, hope. And hope does not disappoint us, because God has poured out his love into our hearts by the Holy Spirit, whom he has given us" (Rom. 5:3-5). The peace of God works to fit all of life's experiences together. This peace comes as a by-product of the primary relationship to God.

As the prophet Isaiah declared more than twenty-five hundred years ago,

> You will keep in perfect peace
> him whose mind is steadfast,
> because he trusts in you. (Isa. 26:3)

The pressures of life that pull people, families, and society apart will never go away. The problem of fragmentation lies at the very heart of people and it multiplies at the social level. Yet, we can have peace in the presence of the pressures. Peace has to do with how we respond to the fragmentation of life. Isaiah described a situation in which trust has an impact on the mind which results in peace. An alternative to trust might be anxiety and worry, which lead to fragmentation. Isaiah does not commend generic trust. He would be the last one to encourage generic trust. He had a low view of human behavior. Peace comes from trusting God.

Peace represents an intrinsic characteristic of God. Just as people have skin and hair, God has peace. Peace is an essential aspect of his nature. God has his act together. He is in perfect balance. He tempers justice with mercy, love with holiness. The apostle Paul came to understand how the nature of

God himself affects those who have a relationship to God. Paul experienced all of the wide swings of success and failure, wealth and poverty, sickness and health, popularity and notoriety. Writing from prison as he awaited his inevitable execution, Paul wrote to the Philippians about how they could experience peace in their lives instead of the gnawing anxiety we often face. He said, "Do not be anxious about anything, but in everything, by prayer and petition, with thanksgiving, present your requests to God. And the peace of God, which transcends all understanding, will guard your hearts and your minds in Christ Jesus" (Phil. 4:6-7).

He does not promise that God will take away the problems. Instead, he explains that the experience of communication and relationship with God will affect how we experience the tornness of life. The peace of God guards our hearts and minds in Christ Jesus. Paul does not speak of peace in generic terms as an independent quality. Instead, he speaks specifically of the peace of God which has the power to hold our reason and emotions together during times of stress. The nature of God holds us together in Christ Jesus.

The phrase "in Christ Jesus" almost looks like a throwaway line. It appears so often in the New Testament we learn to ignore it, like the introductions to Paul letters, or the long genealogical tables in Matthew and Luke. Yet, in the New Testament this little phrase explains it all. All of the seeming benefits of what Christians call salvation come as a by-product of the relationship to Christ. Those in Christ have the capacity for experiencing the peace of God because of the relationship to God by Christ. Just before he left his disciples to go and pray in the garden before the guards came to take him away to his execution, Jesus said, "I have told you these things, so that in me you may have peace. In this world you will have trouble. But take heart! I have overcome the world" (John 16:33).

In the hours that followed, Jesus modeled the meaning and source of peace. As he prayed in the garden, he experienced the tornness that comes from conflict. He did not want to experience the horrible death by crucifixion that awaited him. On the other hand, he wanted to fulfill his mission. Often in life we do not want to deal with the consequences of free moral choice, arguing that if choice has a consequence, then it cannot be free. In the course of prayer, however, Jesus experienced the peace of God which transcends all understanding.

The postmodern person hopes that by avoiding conflict, moral judgment, and decisions, he or she can experience peace. Yet, the underlying causes of fragmentation will remain. The reasons we have the capacity for moral decision remain in the human nature and express themselves in social relationships. People lie. People gossip. People manipulate. Until the underlying problem disappears, the pressures for alienation and fragmentation will continue.

We have nothing to offer the postmodern world in terms of organizations, programs, institutions, and structures. What we have to offer is a concrete basis for peace in a fragmented world. We have a Savior to offer, not a tradition. We must never be confused about what it is that we offer and what it is they need. They never need another demand. They need a Savior who will put their house in order. Then they will be in a position to deal with all the demands, all the conflicts, and all the fragmenting issues of life that are going to come.

PART TWO

POLITICALLY ALIENATED

Authority tends to operate impersonally with the potential for conflict and violence. Ideology accents the differences between people. Thus, ideology promotes conflict and fragmentation.

The death of ideology has its counterpart in the rejection of authority. No cause seems worthy. No leader seems worthy. People do not owe allegiance to institutions or employers. Traditional values have no claim on people that grasps their imagination. And why should people feel an obligation to follow the ruler of this present darkness?

The church has an incredible opportunity to present Christ as the one worthy to follow. Those churches that have made great strides in reaching baby boomers and busters find that this group, which has rejected authority, most loves to sing about the exalted Christ who holds all dominion as Lord. Postmodernity has not rejected the authority of Christ, because most of those growing up in this new age have never heard of him. They have rejected what they have seen, but they are actually on a quest to find a worthy authority.

The modern world had no binding ideological interpretation of reality, but it had many which claimed to be the truth: fascism, Communism, capitalism. During the modern age Christianity has had its share of ideologies that glorified an aspect of the truth to the exclusion of other dimensions of truth: Calvinism, Arminianism, Pietism, Pentecostalism, Puritanism, dispensationalism, fundamentalism, modernism, Evangelicalism, Higher Criticism.

The failure of ideology opens a door for the gospel, because the gospel has filled the void before in times of major cultural upheaval. There is an opportunity, but there is also a danger. The danger for the church in this time of upheaval is in its preference to preach the old culture rather than the old, old story.

CHAPTER FOUR

TRUST NO ONE OVER THIRTY: AUTHORITY

Augustine invented Christendom in the early fifth century when he wrote *The City of God*. This book describes an earthly city and a heavenly city. The difference between the two lies in the fact that the earthly city is not and never can be the city of God. Oddly enough, Christendom is built on the opposite idea: the earthly city must become the city of God. This view became a blueprint for the feudal system and the lines of authority within the medieval world. It was the basis for civil and ecclesiastical authority for a thousand years. Within what had been the old Roman Empire, some renegades in the west first divided the authority. The renegades were the patriarch of the church in Rome and a barbarian prince who presumed the title of Roman Emperor. The real emperor was in Constantinople where the universal patriarch was and where the patriarchs of all of the sees of the divisions of the Christian church met, but in the west, from the perspective of the east, there were some renegades who had usurped authority. Out of this claim to authority the division between the eastern Empire and the Holy Roman Empire, between the eastern church and the Roman church developed. In the west where there was no rival, the emperor and the pope managed to develop this sense of feudalism and who owed obligation to whom.

The first glimmers of the modern age came with the thirteenth century when the emperor of the Holy Roman Empire and the pope quarreled over who had the ultimate authority: the pope or the emperor. Major conflict developed between these two heads of authority, but different kinds of conflict were going on throughout Christendom, throughout the whole feudal system. The barons of England rebelled against King John in 1215 forcing him to sign the Magna Carta granting to them certain rights. The election of the popes became so political that at one point during the late Middle Ages Rome had three different popes. The English Parliament executed King Charles I for treason in 1648. They later deposed his son, James II, in 1688. The French executed their king in 1789. The Russians executed their czar in 1917. All through this period, authority gradually shifted from monarchs and popes to the people. It was a change in orientation as to where the authority lay.

As the modern age grew and developed, great political, educational, philanthropic institutions emerged. Civic organizations, hospitals, private colleges, symphony orchestras, museums, public libraries, political parties, environmental groups, civil rights groups, evangelistic ministries all emerged. People developed them to meet specific needs and generally oriented them toward care of the broad community. In some way, these great institutions were meant to benefit the large group. There was an outward orientation of people taking care of people in a variety of different areas. In the modern age we saw the development of causes, major causes of concern to which people became adherents, devoted followers, usually following some leader who rallied the group to the cause. In championing this development of authority and the theory of where authority lay, people like John Locke, Thomas Jefferson, Rousseau, and Thomas Payne championed democracy without an interfering God. Other people like Adolf Hitler and Mao Tse-tung championed dictatorship as a positive good without an interfering God.

In the modern age God became unnecessary for the body politic, and power lay with the people. It came from the people, and it was in their power to exercise authority. With all of this going on, Christianity also became wrapped up in the modern quest for authority after the collapse of the old feudal Christendom system. With the Catholic church, there was a resolution that authority lay with the pope. With the Protestant church, there was a resolution that authority lay in the Bible on earth. Both churches would say that final authority lay with God in heaven, but on earth the responsibility remained for someone or some way to administer authority. This condition existed as the modern world emerged from the Reformation. Over time we see a situation in which Catholic laity may acknowledge the pope as titular head of the church. They may maintain many questions and doubts while practicing as they please on an individual basis, regardless of what the official position of the church may be with respect to questions like birth control, abortion, divorce, and a number of other questions that are important to the Catholic church. Protestants moving through the modern age, questioned the reliability of Scripture based on the growing influence of modern ways of knowing; such as empiricism and rationalism. The development of higher criticism and attitudes toward Scripture that would be quite different from the Reformation Protestant attitudes toward Scripture shook the Protestant understanding of authority. While all of this was happening, the church was exercising less and less influence in the cultural life and civic affairs of Western nations. It was present, but it was on the periphery. That is where we find ourselves today: present but on the periphery.

The postmodern generation has rejected allegiance to any external authorities. There is no sense of loyalty, obligation, duty, or civic responsibility to organizations or governmental structures. Whereas Christendom concentrated authority in the head and modernity concentrated authority in the people, postmodernity sees authority only in the isolated individual. That isolated aspect is an important part of the experience of the postmodern person. They are not interested in institutions or organizations. This situation has profound implications for philanthropic organizations of all kinds. Postmodern people are not joiners. Most young people have gone through this stage. We see the prodigal son going through this stage of rejection of parental authority. Typically one of the life crises of the adolescent is the assertion of independence and the separation from parental authority. We see the same thing going on in the life of Jacob when he tricked his father, Isaac, which was an unthinkable kind of thing to do in that culture at that time—to trick the father for the birthright. This sort of thing has gone on for ages and ages, but typically people grow out of it.

What we see now is more than just a generation going through a phase of rejecting authority as a group, which is what the baby boomers did. There was such a huge number of people going through it all at the same time, in a time of mass communication, that it was not an isolated matter. It became a mass matter, and it established a culture known as the *youth culture*. Some people call it the Peter Pan Syndrome, or perpetual adolescence, which has implications for commitment. Another of the crises of adolescence is the ability to develop the capability of intimacy and commitment. That ability has powerful implications for whether or not someone can enter into and maintain a marriage relationship. The baby boomers went through this experience together. The baby busters have gone through this same experience together, and the echo-boom is going through it. These multiple generations have been locked in this attitude since the 1960s.

The counterculture of the 1960s produced such phrases as "Don't trust anyone over thirty." We saw national scandals that emphasized and reinforced this attitude occurring on a regular flow from Vietnam to Watergate to the televangelist scandals of the 1980s. It was fed by the regular, routine failure of leadership at the national level in politics, in business, in religion, in virtually every sphere of life. The postmodern generation would be a generation of people who as children grew up without heroes. They had no one to look up to, and oftentimes grew up without parents or with only one parent in the home. They never fully experienced, relationally, a positive model of authority relationship.

THE COLLAPSE OF MORAL AUTHORITY

The collapse of moral authority in the United States came gradually but steadily after World War II. The aims of the Allies in their crusade against fascism created a climate in which the "free" world rallied to the leadership of Churchill and Roosevelt. During the early days of the Cold War, the choices all seemed clear and the cause of democracy noble. The collapse of moral authority did not come because people consciously rejected morality. On the contrary, it emerged as a slowly growing cynical reaction to the inconsistencies and methods of democracy in its battle with Communism.

Joseph McCarthy led the fight to uncover Communists in the government and entertainment industry. The methods of McCarthy, however, left the public feeling sick over the way innocent lives could so easily be ruined. The cavalier way that the United States intruded into the affairs of small nations heightened the cynicism as people began to realize that military dictatorship, civil war, and assassination fit as easily with American tactics as with Russian tactics. The pragmatic view that "the ends justify the means" tarnished the nobility of the cause. Instead of fighting for freedom as the rhetoric of World War II suggested, it became apparent by the 1960s that America was only interested in its "strategic national interests." In other words, the United States was out for itself even though it tended to cloak its adventures in terms of the old rhetoric.

We set up puppet governments like that of Diem in Vietnam and then, just as easily, conspired their overthrow. America grew more jaded as the Vietnam war dragged on. Nixon promised a secret peace plan if he were elected, and he succeeded in ending American involvement in the war. The plan turned out to be a promise to withdraw from Vietnam, and to sweeten the deal the United States cut off support for the South Vietnamese government.

The 1970s and 1980s witnessed similar episodes of American involvement in the affairs of other countries based on pragmatism rather than conviction. In the Iran-Contra scandal, the United States outdid itself in duplicity. Congress had cut off funds to support the Contra insurgency in Nicaragua. The

United States also supported Iraq in the war with Iran. The United States had an arms embargo against Iran while protecting oil freighters in the Persian Gulf doing business with Iraq. To raise money to fund the Contras, we sold weapons to Iran. This kind of behavior at all levels of government characterized the climate in which the rejection of authority emerged.

The collapse of moral authority in government occurred while a comparable collapse of moral authority in the religious world took place. Evangelical Christianity became almost synonymous with the Republican Party during the 1980s. Jerry Falwell's Moral Majority organization linked conservative Christianity with the political establishment at a time when Americans increasingly viewed politics in the United States as morally and spiritually bankrupt. While the leaders of the religious right had the motive of providing a moral compass for the country, they undermined their own goals by adapting a methodology for acquiring authority that Americans viewed with increasing cynicism.

To make matters worse, several of the most visible leaders of conservative Christianity created a series of scandals. The combination of political power, big money, and media popularity provided a context ripe for disaster. Financial and sexual scandal exploded on the national scene. Oral Roberts drew major attention in his efforts to raise his hospital and medical college in Tulsa from financial ruin. In a television broadcast he suggested that if he did not raise the multimillion dollar shortfall within a matter of days, then God would call him home. The secular media jumped on the manipulative tactic. Political cartoons were savage as they represented God holding Oral Roberts for ransom.

The PTL Club scandal lasted longer and proved more devastating. It began in 1987 when Jim Bakker abruptly resigned from the leadership of PTL with the announcement of his marital infidelity. Jimmy Swaggart led the criticism of Bakker from his own nationally syndicated TV ministry. In time the scandal would lead to the disclosure of misuse of funds amounting to millions of dollars. It would also be followed by Swaggart's own sex scandal. At the time, the impact of these scandals tended to be evaluated in terms of declining income and viewers for the ministries involved. It is more difficult to assess how the scandals affected the moral authority of religion in general and Christianity in particular. The media and political ministries succeeded in making Christianity a big force to be reckoned with in the rough and tumble of politics and TV ratings. Christianity became big business. Unfortunately, this big business went by the name of "televangelism" and confused the message of the gospel with the politics and the glitz of the industry. The headline for an editorial in *Christianity Today* in their December 15, 1989, issue summed up the disaster: "Epitaph for the

Eighties: The decade that was supposed to revive the nation's morality put televangelists on the 'dishonor roll' instead."[1] Media Christianity became a favorite target for jokes on late-night television. The emerging postmodern generation did not reject the moral authority of the only exposure to Christianity they ever had. They never encountered any moral authority from that source. Broad cultural cynicism told them all they needed to know about religion.

THE DANGER TO RELATIONSHIPS

In rejecting external authority, people reject the possibility for significant ongoing relationship with other people. Authority provides a basis for maintaining order in a social setting. At the large community level, it provides the basis for government and the protection of people against violence. The rejection of external authority and of caring concern for the community have long served as essential elements to the definition of a criminal personality. Without external authority, society breaks down and a variety of forms of violence occur.

With the rejection of authority goes the personal discipline necessary to maintain relationships. Membership in organizations, public service, effective volunteer work, and marriage create obligations that require discipline. Sometimes the discipline means showing up somewhere at the right time, or showing up regularly at the same time. Sometimes the discipline has an affect on our finances due to the expectation that we will give money to the cause.

Marriage requires a significant exercise of discipline. It requires the partners to take each other into consideration before making a decision about virtually anything. It means controlling one's temper. It means taking the time to talk about little things when we could use the time "more productively." It means controlling our use of time. It means controlling our behavior with members of the opposite sex. It means thinking about what we are going to say before we speak. Marriage cannot survive without the acceptance of the restraints that the marriage promises create. Without submitting to the discipline of marriage, people cannot fulfill the vows of marriage. The disastrous divorce rate in the United States suggests the extent to which marriage has no more authority than joining a book club. It may be convenient for a time, but it creates no obligation.

By rejecting the sense of discipline necessary to engage in committed relationship, we also abandon the concept of personal responsibility. Without a sense of responsibility, we have the luxury of placing blame for everything somewhere else. The phrase "not my fault" comes to mind.

Without a sense of responsibility people settle into a state of apathy. The concepts of obligation and duty have no place in the experience of the post-modern person. They have grown up without this orientation. Through the popular culture irresponsibility has always been presented to them as charming. By rejecting authority, people reject the teaching that helps create a sense of responsibility. With this factor missing from life, a person feels no responsibility for others, for society, or for themselves. Other than the isolated gut feeling of the moment, people who have rejected all external authority and feel no sense of responsibility have also excluded from themselves the capacity of caring.

This denial of caring comes out in the rejection of authority when people reject rules or norms of behavior. This rejection of the rules of behavior happens to some extent every day when people violate traffic laws. In our neighborhood we have a long street with two stop signs, which young people completely ignore. They race along without even slowing down, because they do not see the need for the stop signs. I have two little girls, and I see the need to slow people down. When people run the stop signs, I do not usually think about the contempt for the law so much as I think about how little people care about the safety of my children.

Ultimately, the social and legal norms of behavior have to do with caring about other people as well as learning to care about yourself. The norms of social behavior are sometimes referred to as manners, politeness, etiquette, and civility. These rules of social behavior stand in contrast to other common forms of social behavior; such as vulgarity, rudeness, harassment, rape, abuse, insensitivity, racism, and inconsideration. Every society develops norms of behavior to protect people from the kind of uncaring irresponsibility that characterizes people who have lost the discipline necessary to function in society without doing violence and pain to others.

When we reject all external authority, we do great damage to ourselves. When my daughter was a little girl, I used to tell her the old European fairy tales that all end with the beautiful young girl marrying the prince. As a father who did not want his brilliant daughter growing up thinking that happiness depended upon her marrying a handsome prince, I would always add, "But you don't want to marry any old prince, Rebecca. We've thrown off the yoke of tyranny!" On one occasion, Rebecca smiled and replied, "Yeah, Daddy. Now we're our own tyranny." She was so right. When we make ourselves our sole authority, we submit to the reign of a tyrant who cares nothing about us. When we reject authority, we cut ourselves off from significant interaction with other people and the kinds of relationships we crave.

I have lived most of my life in the South, but I have lived elsewhere as well. When I was in high school, I lived on my own in Washington where I was a page in the United States Senate. When I was engaged in doctoral studies, I lived for a time in Oxford. I also taught for a while in Minnesota. Through those experiences, I have learned that people in the English-speaking world have different concepts of polite behavior. The "rules" change depending on the culture.

While reading English Puritan history with Barrie White at Regent's Park College of Oxford University, I always used the term of respect, sir, when speaking to him. I always said "Yes, sir" and "No, sir." One day one of the English students asked me why I addressed Dr. White as "sir." "It sounds so servile," he argued. "No one talks that way except to the Prince of Wales." Southern tradition insists that I say *sir* and *ma' am* to anyone in authority and as a matter of respect to someone older than I. Just how much older than I becomes a matter of intuition. No rule exists for knowing who deserves the title and who does not.

The authority of tradition depends upon personal relationships. The elderly had the primary responsibility for passing on the tradition. Of course, parents played their part as teachers, but the real authority lay elsewhere. My parents could teach me how to act and how to talk, but power of tradition does not lie in the transmission of the information, but in its acceptance. Why do people accept the tradition and make it a part of their lives as they live it out? Ultimately, the power of tradition does not lie in community sanction or taboo. It depends upon personal relationship. We appropriate the values and behaviors of the people most important to us.

I will never forget watching television with my grandmother forty years ago. A commercial came on in which a husband waited impatiently in the car honking the horn while his wife continued to get dressed in the house. My grandmother spoke gently but with finality to me and my brother, "I do not want to ever hear of you boys honking your horn for a lady. You must go to the door and wait until she is ready." My grandmother made known her expectation of how to show respect. Whether or not the tradition continued from one generation to the next depended upon my personal regard for my grandmother.

I grew up in the house my grandparents built in the town in which my family has lived since before the Revolutionary War. I grew up around old people who lived into their nineties. Manners, politeness, and civility grew out of personal relationship with them. It was always a matter of a living tradition because it grew out of personal relationship. None of it was a matter of rules as rules by themselves. It all came down to the matter of how to treat people and how to show respect for people. Over the years I have noticed the difference between those who only learned the rules and those who continued the tradition. The rules create a snare for trapping people when we catch them off base. The rules create social barriers and a mechanism for establishing elitism. The tradition, on the other hand, exists to protect people from embarrassment and to show respect for all people.

One socially advantaged girl of our town a few years older than I knew all the rules but had no interest in the tradition. She used the rules like a club to bully and manipulate. At six o'clock she informed her husband, "It's time for a cocktail." When he made the unfortunate blunder of replying, "I don't care for a cocktail tonight," she replied with force, "Honey, I said it is time for a cocktail." So, he had a cocktail. The rules had no particular grounding or purpose, and she could not distinguish the difference between morality and choice of fabric for a spring day. Because her rule for moral behavior was based on "what would the neighbors think?" she had no basis for moral decision when she realized that the neighbors did not think about her at all.

The postmodern generation may have heard some of the rules. By and large, the rules seem foolish when cut off from a living tradition. The postmodern generation has not so much rejected the authority of tradition. Instead, they have never been a part of the living tradition. They do not know old people. They have not lived with old people and heard their stories. Apart from the stories, the tradition is only rules. Apart from the personal relationship, people have no reason to appropriate the tradition.

ACCEPTING THE AUTHORITY OF CHRIST

Where does that leave us in relating to postmodern people? It is important to remember that in rejecting authority, they have become not anarchists but cynics. The postmodern person does not so much desire the overthrow of government as not care about government. They represent the full flower of disillusionment and disappointment. They have not actually rejected Christ, because they have never heard of Christ. They have rejected authority, organizations, and movements as they have experienced them. They have rejected what they have seen.

Leaders often mistakenly believe that they have authority because of their position, rank, or power. A person may have all of these and still lack authority. Authority ultimately involves the claim of something or someone on the life of another. Loyalty to a cause or person relates to the idea of authority. People, organizations, causes, and nations have no automatic claim upon another person. It does not exist by right or decree. People decide who or what has authority over their lives. We have no control over who has power over our lives, but we have total control over who or what, if anything at all, has authority over our lives.

The marriage ceremony represents the surrender of autonomy. It is possible to say the words of the vow without surrendering autonomy and submitting to the authority of marriage and all the responsibilities and obligations it creates. Authority has no power to force submission. It does not work that way. The recognition of authority comes from within a person as the appropriate response to what they regard as having authority over their life. In that sense, something stronger than mere brute power and force operates with the surrender of autonomy to some external authority. When a person enters into marriage without surrendering their autonomy, then selfishness has the upper hand in motivating behavior. When a person does surrender their autonomy, however, then love has the upper hand. From a Christian perspective, marriage involves mutual surrender in which two autonomous people surrender to each other and agree to become one.

In describing love, as opposed to passion, in any relationship, the apostle Paul explained the extent to which love has authority over the conduct of life:

> Love is patient, love is kind. It does not envy, it does not boast, it is not proud. It is not rude, it is not self-seeking, it is not easily angered, it keeps no record of wrongs. Love does not delight in evil but rejoices with the truth. It always protects, always trusts, always hopes, always perseveres. (1 Cor. 13:4-7)

Love is not a theoretical or philosophical concept even though it can be discussed and described theoretically and philosophically. Love represents a holistic dynamic of emotion, intellect, will, and behavior directed toward a person or persons. Love cannot be forced any more than authority can. A person loves as the appropriate response to another person or persons.

When Jesus Christ walked the dusty streets and roads of Palestine two thousand years ago, he had no formal authority. He had no rank, position, or power. He had neither title nor dignity. He had neither wealth nor influence within the power structure. Yet, he had great authority. One of the first observations that people made of Jesus after he began his teaching ministry concerned the fact that "he taught them as one who had authority, not as the teachers of the law" (Mark 1:22). During the modern era, the authority of the church has been similar to that of the authority of the scribes of antiquity. Their authority related to their official position within society. Jesus had a different kind of authority which attached to him personally. His authority operated at the physical, spiritual, and interpersonal level. He healed people physically, and he cleansed them of unclean spirits (Matt. 8:14-17). He spoke, and the waves on the Sea of Galilee responded to him (Matt. 8:25-27). He called people to follow him, and they did (Matt. 9:9). Even the demons obeyed him when he ordered them to leave people alone (Matt. 8:28-34).

The question of formal authority and personal authority appear in stark contrast when the religious "authorities" confronted Jesus about the source of his authority (Matt. 21:23). They had no doubt that he exercised authority, but it differed from their kind of authority. Some said that Jesus had authority because he was in league with the devil (Matt. 12:24)! The demons, on the other hand, recognized him immediately as the "Son of the Most High God" (Mark 5:7; Luke 8:28). People, it would seem, had the freedom to submit to his authority or not. The spirits, however, could not help submitting, for they knew him. The personal authority was inescapable.

In this present age, postmodern people accept the power of government over their lives with cynical fatalism. They acknowledge the reality of formal authority. In the matter of voluntary associations, like churches, civic clubs, the Daughters of the American Revolution, they do not have to join. For the most part, they have opted out. They do not see the point. They do not see what difference it makes for them. They do not want to be obligated to something that does not matter. Organizations do not have the compelling personal authority for postmodern people that would cause them to surrender their lives, or even a part of their lives, to the organizations.

The authority of Jesus rests in who he is. The demons expressed it their own way in begging not to be cast into the abyss. Jesus expressed it another way when he said "But I, when I am lifted up from the earth, will draw all men to myself" (John 12:32). The apostle Paul said it this way:

> Therefore God exalted him to the highest place
>   and gave him the name that is above every name,
> that at the name of Jesus every knee should bow,
>   in heaven and on earth and under the earth,
> and every tongue confess that Jesus Christ is Lord,
>   to the glory of God the Father. (Phil. 2:9-11)

In Jesus Christ we see the melding together of both formal and personal authority. He has the formal authority related to position, power, dignity, and title. Yet, he also has the kind of personal authority to which people willingly submit based solely on who he is within himself.

Jesus preferred to speak of himself as the "Son of Man." This title forms the basis for his claim to formal authority. To our ears in the twenty-first century, it sounds like a reference to his humanity, but to first-century ears it represented a claim to the fulfillment of the prophecy found in Daniel:

> "In my vision at night I looked, and there before me was one like a son of man, coming with the clouds of heaven. He approached the Ancient of Days and was led into his presence. He was given authority, glory and sovereign power; all

peoples, nations and men of every language worshiped him. His dominion is an everlasting dominion that will not pass away, and his kingdom is one that will never be destroyed." (Dan. 7:13-14)

This mysterious figure appeared to be just another human, but he shared with God something that God shares with no one: his authority, glory, and power. Not only that, but he receives the thing that God has forbidden people to give to anyone but God: worship. We tend to forget that Jesus was condemned by the authorities not for claiming to be the Son of God (a title used by the kings of Israel to indicate that they received the favor of God), but for claiming to be the Son of Man (Matt. 26:64; Mark 14:62; Luke 22:67-69). By claiming to be the Son of Man, he made himself equal with God, sharing his glory, sovereignty, authority, and worship. All of these matters relate to the formal authority of Christ, which he exercises whether people willingly respond or not. The irony of the Son of Man is that he did not present himself in power and dignity when he appeared to the world. Instead, he presented himself in weakness. The earlier passage that cites Paul's description of the authority of Jesus does not begin with the evidence of formal authority. Instead, he explains the basis for the personal authority of Christ:

> Who, being in very nature God,
>   did not consider equality with God something to be grasped,
> but made himself nothing,
>   taking the very nature of a servant,
>   being made in human likeness.
> And being found in appearance as a man,
>   he humbled himself
>   and became obedient to death—even death on a cross! (Phil. 2:6-8)

In short, Jesus did not use his formal authority to cause submission to him, but he established his personal authority to which people have freely submitted.

The cynicism of the postmodern generation is nothing new. Some people say that it characterizes French culture. Jesus encountered it with his own disciples. When he prepared to go to Bethany following the death of Lazarus, he met resistance and cynicism from his disciples:

> Then he said to his disciples, "Let us go back to Judea."
> "But Rabbi," they said, "a short while ago the Jews tried to stone you, and yet you are going back there?"
> Jesus answered, "Are there not twelve hours of daylight? A man who walks by day will not stumble, for he sees by this world's light. It is when he walks by night that he stumbles, for he has no light."

After he had said this, he went on to tell them, "Our friend Lazarus has fall-en asleep; but I am going there to wake him up."

His disciples replied, "Lord, if he sleeps, he will get better." Jesus had been speaking of his death, but his disciples thought he meant natural sleep.

So then he told them plainly, "Lazarus is dead and for your sake I am glad I was not there, so that you may believe. But let us go to him."

Then Thomas (called Didymus) said to the rest of the disciples, "Let us also go, that we may die with him." (John 11:7-16)

The cynical response of Thomas betrays a basic outlook on life. He had no confidence for the future. He had no hope.

The idea of hope has a direct relationship to one's attitude toward author-ity. It mixes with feelings of confidence in leadership to bring about positive change and to make a way into the future. Cynicism represents a complete-ly different attitude toward life. A cynic is someone who has reconciled to despair and hopelessness. It is worse than hopelessness, because the hope-less at least know that they have no hope. The cynic does not even know that hope is a possibility.

Thomas would follow Jesus to Bethany, but not because he thought Jesus could do anything. Jesus had personal authority over the life of Thomas. He would follow him, but he did not think it would make any difference. They had each other. They had a relationship. At this point Thomas did not have confidence in the formal authority of Jesus. After the Resurrection, Thomas, known to history as "Doubting Thomas," would bow to Jesus and recognize his formal authority with the confession, "My Lord and my God!" (John 20:28).

Postmodern people have the capacity for loyalty to individuals, but they have little confidence in power structures, big organizations, titles, and the egos that go with them. They have little hope. They have largely reconciled themselves to hopelessness. When I began my ministry as a prison chaplain at the Kentucky State Reformatory, I was totally unprepared for what lay ahead. Principal Chaplain Jim Dent wisely gave me instructions not to do anything for two months. During those two months I tagged along with Chaplain Darrell Rollins who knew the ropes. He knew how to recognize a con; but he also told me, "Hal, if you don't get conned at least once a day, you're not doing your job." He also helped me understand hope. Hope is not like a wish. Hope is real. It is not a matter of looking at life through rose-colored glasses. Hope exists in spite of how bad things are. Hope is a gift from God in the darkness, and God always gives us a concrete reason for hope. The rainbow is a visible reminder of hope.

In the face of cynicism, the Resurrection represents the ultimate basis for human hope. Death represents the ultimate expression of human futility and grounds for despair. The Resurrection demonstrates the power of God to make a difference in the future, regardless of how things appear in the present. In the midst of the greatest defeat and darkness, God gives the lie to cynicism. He demonstrated his authority over creation in the Resurrection and vindicated Jesus publicly.

In the present moment we do not see how Jesus Christ exercises his authority over all of creation. We continue to live in a fallen world governed by Murphy's Law: what can go wrong will go wrong; of all the things that could go wrong, the worst of all possible will go wrong; no good deed goes unpunished. Though he exercises formal authority over creation, people experience Christ most consciously through his personal authority, as Hebrews observes:

> In putting everything under him, God left nothing that is not subject to him. Yet at present we do not see everything subject to him. But we see Jesus, who was made a little lower than the angels, now crowned with glory and honor because he suffered death, so that by the grace of God he might taste death for everyone. (Heb. 2:8-9)

What we know of Christ, we do not know from seeing his formal power, glory, and dignity. On the contrary, we know of Christ through his humility and personal character expressed through his actions and teachings. We see someone with tremendous personal moral authority who now has the formal authority to make a difference and provide hope for the future.

The postmodern generation's rejection of authority coupled with a disinterest in belonging to formal organizations and groups stands in conflict with a basic human need to belong. People have rejected an authority that they judged morally bankrupt and politically spent, only to subject themselves to another authority even worse. The French rejected the authority of a king during the French Revolution only to subject themselves to the authority of the Reign of Terror. The Russians rejected the authority of the czar only to subject themselves to the authority of the Communist dictatorship of Lenin and Stalin. The fact that the postmodern generation has grown cynical about leaders and organizations does not mean that leaders and organizations are a thing of the past. It means they are looking, yearning for something. The Germans deposed the kaiser after World War I and found a new leader in Adolf Hitler. We stand in a most dangerous yet opportune moment in time in which an entire generation is yearning for someone worthy to follow.

By presenting himself in human form, assuming the role of a servant, and dying for us, Jesus Christ revealed himself as someone worth following. The great hymn of the entourage of God in the book of Revelation deals with this theme of the worthiness of Christ:

"You are worthy, our Lord and God,
    to receive glory and honor and power,
for you created all things,
    and by your will they were created
    and have their being.

"You are worthy to take the scroll
    and to open its seals,
because you were slain,
    and with your blood you purchased men for God
    from every tribe and language and people and nation.
You have made them to be a kingdom and priests to serve our God,
    and they will reign on the earth.

"Worthy is the Lamb who was slain,
to receive power and wealth and wisdom and strength
and honor and glory and praise!"

"To him who sits on the throne and to the Lamb
be praise and honor and glory and power,
    for ever and ever!" (Rev. 4:11; 5:9-10, 12, 13*b*)

It is possible to hold formal authority, yet not be worthy of worship and praise. Through the gospel we understand that Jesus Christ not only has the authority, but he is worthy of the authority.

At critical stages in the life of the church over the last two thousand years, a new hymnody has emerged. Usually associated with periods of renewal, the development of new music reflects a renewed sense of the immediacy of Christ in the lives of people. It happened with the Gregorian chant. It happened with the songs of Francis of Assisi and Bernard of Clairvaux. It happened with the Reformation hymns of Luther and the Great Awakening hymns of Wesley. Today we see what may be a minor blip on the musical horizon or a great change in the direction of church music with the contemporary choruses and worship songs. They have had great popularity with the postmodern generation while receiving tremendous criticism for lacking the great theological themes of the Reformation. It does not take very close examination, however, to recognize that the contemporary songs have an overwhelming preoccupation with the authority of the exalted Christ over all people and creation. They sing songs like:

        "He Is Lord"
        "He Is Exalted"
        "Our God Is a Mighty God"

The theological concern of the songs strikes at this central issue of post-modernity. When postmodern people become Christians, they want to sing about the Christ to whom they have submitted. They want to sing about the true and final authority for their lives who offers hope and a future. They want to sing about the one in all creation who is worthy to be followed.

We hope we can remember that we do not offer an organization, though there is a tendency for Christians in their evangelism not to present Christ but to present their church. The invitation is not to know Christ, but to come hear our pastor, which means "Come join our organization"; "We want your money"; "We want you to do our work for us"; "We want you to bolster our sagging membership roles." The invitation to join the club is not an offer, it is a demand. The "organizational church" offers nothing to the postmodern person. In presenting a clear picture of Jesus Christ, however, we offer someone whose personal authority makes a claim on people that offers them a future. It is not necessary to convince these people that they ought to become joiners and recognize authority. It is only necessary to introduce them to Jesus Christ without whom no authority has legitimacy.

CHAPTER FIVE

WHATEVER: IDEOLOGY

As has been suggested, the counterculture was not so much ideological as it was emotional and sensory. The young people wrapped up in it reacted against the prevailing culture and its ideology. The twentieth century was a century of ideological competition as a variety of politicoeconomic systems vied for the allegiance of the human race. The systems offered a new integrating "truth" that transcended ethnic, racial, and national boundaries. They arose from the collapse of imperial monarchy after World War I. Until then a few empires controlled most of the world. A century earlier they had controlled the Western hemisphere, but as they lost control of the Americas, they gained dominance in Africa and Asia.

As Christendom began to fade, ideology helped give form to the new modern era. In the late–Middle ages, the peasants revolted in a number of different regions in England, France, Germany, and Italy. Religious belief and political aspiration flowed out of Christendom as an interrelated unity. At the end of Christendom, people did not think of religion and politics separately; they were together as one thing. That unity of church and state was part of the legacy of Christendom. We see the Protestant Reformation going forward in relationship to the church, but at the same time the princes of the old Holy Roman Empire were developing the idea of the nation state. Political sovereignty, independence, and the establishment of their own nations developed along with the separation from Rome. These ideas moved forward together. In the English Reformation where the Puritans wanted to go further in a reformation of the Church of England, there was also the political struggle between the divine rights of kings, advocated by the Stewart monarchs, and parliamentary democracy advocated by the House of Commons. Politics and religion were inextricably related as causes of the English Civil War. Historians throw up their hands in trying to distinguish between these different issues. Ideology that called for war and the overthrow of government was often derived from an interpretation of the book of Revelation, as with the Anabaptists of Munster and with the Fifth Monarchy Men of England, who wanted to overthrow Charles II as soon as he got back to England.

With the Enlightenment, however, in the 1700s people no longer needed a religious justification for their political aspirations. The way they thought no longer required God to be involved in the affairs of nations. Deists like Thomas Jefferson made vague references to God and a natural order, but the French Revolutionaries could carry out their aims without any polite reference to God at all.

Monarchy had emerged over seven thousand years of recorded history as the political system of choice. The Greek city-states experimented with a form of democracy three thousand years ago. Rome had ended monarchy before the birth of Christ, only to take it up again. England abolished monarchy in 1644 only to take it up again in 1660. The French abolished their monarchy and, like the English before them, cut off the head of their king. Like the English before them, however, they returned to monarchy with first an emperor and then a king. In 1848 they threw off monarchy again, only to turn a second time to an emperor before ending monarchy for the third time in 1870. The Chinese revolution of 1911 ended the ancient monarchy. The great collapse of monarchy, however, finally came with the disaster of World War I. All over the world at the beginning of the twentieth century, virtually the entire world was controlled by a very small number of global empires. By the end of the twentieth century, those empires had fragmented to more than two hundred member nations in the United Nations.

At the beginning of World War I monarchy was the dominant form of government, and women played no part in politics. Great empires with majestic dynasties played a personal game of international politics. The czar ruled the Russian Empire as an absolute autocrat. The sultan ruled the Ottoman Turk Empire of the Middle East. The emperor ruled the Chinese Empire. The kaiser of the old Hapsburg dynasty ruled the Austro-Hungarian Empire. The new German kaiser manipulated the newly created quasi-constitutional German Empire. The king-emperor reigned over the constitutional British Empire. The king ruled over the disintegrating Spanish Empire. The smaller kingdoms of Belgium, Holland, Italy, and Denmark controlled smaller, but often very lucrative colonial empires. In the Far East the mikado of Japan ruled the island empire that longed for territorial expansion beyond its Korean possessions and Chinese spheres of influence.

Even the new democracies followed the lead of the old order. Though discarding her emperor, France retained her colonial empire. Even the United States established an empire in the Caribbean, Central America, the Pacific Islands, and the Philippines. It would take fifty years after the end of World War I for the new order to give up most of the colonial empire of the old order.

As monarchy was collapsing, ideology was emerging. In the twentieth century we could call it the struggle of ideology. We saw the emergence of fascism in Germany, Spain, and Italy. We saw the emergence of Communism in Russia and China and their satellite nations. We saw the alliance of the great democracies Great Britain, the United States, and their allied English-speaking people nations (Canada, Australia, and the other Commonwealth nations). It was that tradition, started at Runnymede, that developed into an ideological form of government and economic system known as capitalistic democracy. The battle between political ideologies played out through the rest of the century. Fascism was defeated in its most militant form through war in World War II, but it did not end there. It flourished in Central and South America through the 1950s, 1960s, and the 1970s. It still pops up in Latin America from time to time.

Though the European powers entered World War I to make the world safe for dynastic empires, President Woodrow Wilson promoted the ideal that the allies fought to "make the world safe for democracy." In the same terrible war during which twenty million people lost their lives, the collapse of czarist Russia gave birth to the Soviet Union, a state dedicated to international revolution designed to bring about Communist society. In the chaos left from the political collapse of monarchy in Germany and Austro-Hungary, national socialism would arise to direct the national destiny of the German peoples scattered through a half dozen new nations that appeared on the map. These great systems collided time and again as the century progressed.

With the Spanish Civil War of the 1930s, the world saw on a small scale how seriously the ideologies could compete. The monarchy was overthrown by democracy as in Russia. As in Russia, however, a new competition arose to define the nature of democracy. The meaning of democracy became lost in the competition between fascism and Communism. Thus, Spain became a little theater to practice for the great confrontation of World War II, which ostensibly pitted democracy against fascism.

In the great ideological struggle of the twentieth century, different ideologies defined democracy and fascism in different ways. By *democracy* some meant republican democracy (United States), constitutional monarchical or parliamentary democracy (United Kingdom), or people's democracy (Soviet Union). By *fascism* some meant democratic fascism (Germany), constitutional monarchical fascism (Italy), or imperial military fascism (Japan). Adversaries used similar terms, but they meant entirely different things by those terms. The concept of propaganda became a strategic tool in the conflict between the great ideologies. The Allies defeated the Axis powers in World War II, which redefined the conflict from one between democracy and fascism to one between capitalism and Communism. The former colonies of the old order became the new object of desire in the conflict between Communist Eastern dictatorships and the capitalistic Western democracies. To confuse matters, however, the Western democracies made alliance with fascist military dictatorships and absolutist Middle Eastern monarchies while the Communist dictatorships made alliance with emerging third world democracies.

IDEOLOGY AND IDENTITY

We have seen at the end of the century, the collapse of Communism in almost every country. With trade negotiations going on now between the People's Republic of China and the United States, efforts are being made by the Chinese government to bolster the Hong Kong dollar—a purely capitalistic move. We see the slowly emerging collapse of Communism there, but at the same time we see a weakening of what we were fighting for as a capitalistic democracy. We are facing the greatest moral challenge our ideology has ever had—peace. How do you deal with *peace?* There is no major enemy on the horizon. Who are we against now, why are we against them, and what are we fighting for? Without ideological enemies, in a sense, the United States loses its own identity. Throughout the ideological conflict, the United States had defined itself in opposition to the ideologies. Without them the United States began to lose its own identity. In opposition to fascism and Communism the United States could champion life, liberty, and the pursuit of happiness. Without the challenges to life and liberty, the United States was left with only the pursuit of happiness as its great value.

The echo-boomers who are coming of age now have never known the Communist threat. Throughout the twentieth century we dealt with those early foundational principles of life and liberty. We do not have those struggles anymore. All we have left now is the pursuit of happiness. That is the only value that is left in the United States, because without the struggle, without the suffering, without the challenges, life and liberty are not an issue for the average comfortable person. Being comfortable, we are not concerned with the lack of comfort that other people have. It is the dark side of "I am my only authority," and "I do not care about what is outside of me." In terms of labels like "liberal" and "conservative," the new situation defies the categories we used as recently as the 1980s. Perhaps the situation resembles more the old "isolationism" of an earlier America that did not want to get involved.

Christianity embraced the modern fascination with ideology, often closely identifying itself with a political movement or policy. Though Christ resisted the temptation to solve spiritual problems by political means, the church has continued to return to this methodology, thinking that identification with the powerful forces of earth will advance the kingdom of God. It has never happened. It is nothing new. After failing to reform the Church of England, the Puritans united with Parliament to reform the government of England in 1642. The Evangelicals of England used Parliament in 1832 to pass the Reform Bill. It was a good measure, but they lost their spiritual vitality and gradually disappeared as a significant influence in England after that, as they became so associated with a political movement. Christians made alcohol the issue at the turn of the twentieth century. We passed the Prohibition Bill thinking that alcoholism would disappear from the United States. In the 1950s, anti-Communism was a major church theme. In the 1960s Civil Rights and the anti-war movement became the themes. In the 1980s and 1990s moral issues took center stage. It is nothing new for Christian conservatives or liberals to be involved in politics. It is something we do. It has been part of the modern context that we have carried over from Christendom that the church and the state ought to be one. It is a holdover from a thousand years ago.

Conservative Christians achieved a major political victory through their participation in a coalition that ensured the election of Ronald Reagan and George Bush to the presidency. For twelve years conservative Christians had an ally in the White House from 1981 until 1993. They gained political power but virtually lost any remaining influence they had in the popular culture. Christians stood in the ironic position of achieving political victory but cultural defeat as the counterculture generation went mainstream. Christianity began to look like just another ideology that wanted political power.

The church is gearing up for the culture wars. The fact is the culture war is over, and the church was not involved in it. The church was involved in politics but they missed the culture war. The counterculture began in the 1960s. It involved music, art, literature, television, and every cultural art form. Where was the church in relationship to the culture? Totally removed. We were not involved in the culture war. It is long over. We lost it. We gave it up. If we influence what really matters, which is the culture, then the culture will take care of the politics. But if you try to influence the politicians, you have made a deal with the devil.

Here is my dark side. I helped to train Lee Atwater. The last time I was with Lee Atwater, he was trying to decide which presidential campaign to manage. He had offers from George Bush, who was vice president; Howard Baker, who at that time was no longer majority leader but was chief of staff of the White House; and Jack Kemp who was in Congress. In that conversation, we also talked about the Evangelical Christian Right. He said "We have gotten just about all the good we can out of them, and it is going to be counterproductive to pay too much attention to them in the future." If you look at what actually happened from 1980 to 1997, Christians got nothing of their political agenda, but they lost a great deal. The modern situation reflects what has happened throughout Western history since Constantine. Whenever we have taken the power, we have suffered a major spiritual loss. When the Puritans took power in England, they succeeded in destroying their spiritual vitality. The church in England after 1660 drifted into deism and a loss of influence in society. It did not come back to any strength until the Great Awakening seventy-five years later. It invariably takes an awakening to reverse a secularizing trend.

THE REJECTION OF IDEOLOGY

What does past experience with ideology say for us in the postmodern age? All of this discussion has dealt with the modern age. The postmodern generation, by and large, has rejected ideology and causes. They have drawn back from them. This response appears as apathy and noninvolvement. Campus ministers talk about the fact that the generation now in college are not interested in causes. They are not interested in joining movements. They are not interested in doing, being, or acting the way previous generations did. Ideologies are too big and too impersonal for them. While they have rejected ideology and involvement in organizations, they have not rejected what Christ created the church to be: his bride, which is a relational idea; his family, which is a relational idea; his body, and that is very personal. The church means total identification with Christ. This relational idea is profoundly, I cannot emphasize it enough, profoundly important for this generation. When the church is an organization, when the faith sounds like an ideology, when we confuse the kingdom of this world with the kingdom of God, THEY WILL NOT HEAR US. They will not. The church seems like just another organization. The church sounds like more people wanting my money. The church acts like more people wanting my time. Postmodern people have never been a part of the church. They have never really heard the gospel. They look at us from afar and wonder. No! They do not even wonder. They are not interested. They recognize propaganda and slogans when they hear them. They are media savvy. They are the ones who are driving the more and more sophisticated approaches to advertisements. They know when they are being sold a bill of goods. They grew up in front of the TV. What we have to do with them is get down and get personal.

THE ROLE OF IDEOLOGY

The postmodern generation rejected ideology because it failed to deliver. Ideology has a function within society, and the postmodern generation perceived that it had failed. No one ever called a convention to vote on the success or failure of ideology. The postmodern person simply "dropped out." Causes, movements, politics, and great ideas failed to move them. What does an ideology provide for people that the postmodern generation did not find?

An ideology might simply be described as a body of ideas. Sometimes the ideas fit together tightly and logically into a complete system of thought, like Calvinism. Sometimes the ideas seem more jumbled and loosely connected, like existentialism. One might object to this description with the argument that Calvinism is actually a theology and existentialism is actually a philosophy. Objection noted, but the curious thing about ideology is that it can operate within any sphere of human experience. Marxism may be an economic theory, but few theories have a greater right to the designation of ideology. Democracy is a political theory, but it has had an ideological expression. Freudian psychology merely represents a way of understanding human thought, but for many people it represents an ideology. Ideology can take many different shapes and forms. It can operate in politics, but it can also operate in almost every other field of endeavor. Whenever people think about things, the possibility for ideology exists.

Ideology involves more than merely the collection of ideas. Ideology has a corporate dimension. A collection of ideas only becomes an ideology when it belongs to a group. We may call an ideology by another, less sinister name; such as a "school of thought," or a "literary movement," or simply an "approach." One thing all ideologies have in common, regardless of their field of thought, is the self-understanding of the group that holds to the ideology that they have the truth. An ideology also provides a number of things that people need to survive in the world.

COMMUNITY

First of all, ideology provides community. When we espouse a set of beliefs, we know that all other right-minded people think the way we do. It makes us wonder at all the people who cannot see things the way we do, because, after all, it is all so plain. We do not need to know the other like-minded people personally in order to have a sense of belonging and acceptance. In fact, the very absence of personal connection, the feeling of minority status, can intensify the sense of belonging to something bigger. When people who share an ideology have personal contact, however, they derive strength from each other and develop a strong sense of community. Ideology is a neutral idea that can develop in different ways. Mother Teresa had certain beliefs about the poor and the dying, which other people came to accept. A community of people who shared her ideas grew up around her. We would not want to call her ideas an ideology, because it does not sound nice. Nonetheless, it was an ideology. Adolf Hitler had a growing body of ideas swirling in his head. As soon as others began to listen to him, his ideas became an ideology. He gathered a community of followers who believed they were the master race. In both cases, the body of ideas forms the basis for the community. In the case of Mother Teresa, a small group of people actually lived and worked together. In the case of Hitler, people lived far and wide; but they came together to share their commonly held ideas.

Obviously, personality plays a part in whether or not one person's ideas will ever become an ideology. Why do some great ideas remain buried in books when other limp or wicked ideas become the foundation for major ideologies. A lot depends upon personality and the needs of the people who take up the ideas. Lee Atwater once remarked to me that there was only room for one ideologue in the White House. He spoke purely in terms of power politics and the problems that personalities and factions can cause in trying to run a government; but what he said relates to the idea of a community of believers who rally around the idea. When rivals present alternative ideas, the community vanishes. In the Reagan White House, Atwater spoke of the "true believers." These are the ones who went to Washington to bring about a change in government and carry out the Reagan Revolution. Everyone else on staff was there to get ahead. Atwater did not count himself as a "true believer." He could easily move from the Reagan Team to the Bush Team. Alliances are temporary; ideology is forever.

From a functional perspective, ideology amounts to the same thing as committing oneself to any person, group, organization, or cause. The World War II generation was great at building organizations. They were great ones for group efforts. They carried out the golden age of the civic club. Whether the Junior League or the Jaycees, civic groups flourished through the participation of the World War II generation who had learned the value of group effort through the dark days of the Depression and the war.

We miss the point if we think of the World War II generation as "joiners." They did not join civic groups because they felt a need to belong to a civic group. Joining the civic group provided a way to accomplish the need they felt, but joining an organization was not the need. The organization was a way to accomplish something. An ideology is not just a body of thought. The ideas of an ideology relate to how a person lives, how the world works, how we get from here to the future. At the day-to-day level, organizations provide the mechanism for carrying out an ideology. The World War II generation joined organizations because they cared about something important to the organization. In some way it probably related in a vague way to pieces of an American "ideology" that would include such elements as "get a good education," "work hard and you'll get ahead," "give people a helping hand," "take pride in (fill in the blank)," "the youth are our future," and "give back to the community." Beyond these vague notions of Americanism coming out of the terrible Depression and World War II, others focused on more carefully articulated ideologies of the political left and right that wanted to protect the country from fascism and Communism respectively. People stop joining when they no longer care about what the organizations exist to promote. The postmodern generation did not carry on the tradition of care that mattered to the previous generation. The postmodern generation cares about things, but not things represented by so many of the traditional organizations.

Postmodern people struggle with loyalty or commitment in any form. While they have a strong preference for personal relationship over organizational structure, they struggle with maintaining personal relationships. This trend appears most clearly in the high rate of divorce in Western society. Divorce not only means a separation between husband and wife. It also means a separation of parents and children, the extended family of grandparents, aunts, uncles, and cousins, and a realignment of friendships once shared by husband and wife. Divorce frequently sends families into financial collapse with the wife and children especially thrown into poverty. At some point, we need to ask what has happened to caring. The problem of divorce and the rejection of ideology are two expressions of the same situation.

The ability to care and to make commitments to what we believe in represent a critical task of adolescent development. This critical area of development helps to fit a person for life and the demands of marriage. Without them, a person cannot live responsibly. On the other hand, without a basic belief system, people lack the material for developing a sense of commitment and caring about what matters. A person must first know what matters before they can care about it. The idea of community or personal relationship depends upon basic shared values. Without them, people have only self-interest to carry them through life.

Ideology provides one of the basic needs of self-interest, which is community. But as we have seen, community cannot exist for the person who does not care about what others care about. Without commonly held values, people can only look to their own interests. Ironically, people feel the need for community, but without common values.

A clue to the resolution to the problem lies in how anyone learns values to begin with. Tiny children learn values from the people who care for them. Over a process of many years, children learn to value what others value. In the face of the collapse of ideology, Christians have a unique opportunity to start from scratch. They do not have to combat any ideology as they have tried to do for the last two centuries. They can simply follow the model of Jesus Christ who cared about people until they accepted his basis for community, his model of how the world really works, his understanding of what really matters in the world.

PURPOSE

Second, ideology provides people with a sense of purpose. Ideology sets out a grand understanding of how all of life fits together. This grand explanation of things has been called the "metanarrative." Every ideology has its own metanarrative to explain life. Freud's metanarrative can be reduced to sex and guilt. For Freud, sex and guilt explain virtually all of human life. For Marx the metanarrative focused on the historical dialectic that was driven by economics toward the utopian worker's state. Darwin's metanarrative reduced life to survival of the fittest. Hitler's metanarrative exalted the master race.

The metanarrative of ideology ties all of the strands of thought together to give meaning to life. Sometimes, as with Nietzsche, the meaning of life is that life has no meaning. In an odd way, even this view of life gives people an understanding of where they stand and how they fit in. It may be terribly depressing, but it can be cheerfully expressed by the beer ad that tells us to grab all the gusto we can in life because we only go around once. Of course, most people want life to mean more than grabbing for all the gusto we can. Most people even want life to mean more than the survival of the fittest. Most people think that life must mean something and that life must have some purpose, even if we do not know what it is. The existentialist philosophers have said that this quest for meaning represents one of the three great causes of *angst* (profound anxiety) in life.

People need to feel that life has some purpose and meaning. It strikes at the question of the value of life. This chapter has raised the question of value several times, but we will wait until chapter 9 to explore the postmodern attitude toward values. For the moment, it is enough to say that an ideology embraces the values that make ideas important. Ideas only capture our imagination when they somehow fit into our value system and provide a way for understanding what we value in broad terms. Sometimes we experience a conversion from one ideology to another, which also involves the abandonment of one set of values in exchange for another.

But what about the person who has no clearly defined set of values. The shared values of a community represented by an ideology are not available to the person who does not belong to a community. Without the values, a person will tend to lack the sense of meaning and purpose that an ideology provides. One simple trend in modern society has worked against the postmodern generation ever acquiring a sense of community values. A person needs to belong to a stable community to appropriate the values of the community, but in the United States the average family moves every three years. How can we find our sense of purpose when we live disconnected lives?

The problem did not originate with the postmodern generation. The generation that went through World War I had a gut-wrenching time. The war began with all the romance of a novel by Sir Walter Scott or Robert Louis Stevenson. It ended with the maimed bodies of the wretched survivors of trench warfare and mustard gas. Twenty million people lay buried in the fields of Europe. Ideology failed to make sense of the slaughter. People asked themselves Why? The why question is a search for purpose and meaning. People have the inbred need to ask the question. Most of the American soldiers went home after the war and forgot themselves in the party known as the Roaring Twenties, when people devoted themselves to making money. The few who remained in Europe trying to make sense of it all were the expatriates whom Gertrude Stein named "The Lost Generation."

Every generation struggles with the issue of meaning. Ideology provides a cheap and quick way out of the dilemma. Those who buy into an ideology have all the answers provided to them. The postmodern generation, however, is the media-savvy generation that refuses to buy a bill of goods. They know propaganda when they see it. They also know when an ideology is already spiritually bankrupt and living off past success. The past means nothing to the postmodern generation and nobody knows the future, so they want to know what difference something makes today. In that sense, their ideology is pragmatism. They are true blue Americans through and through.

They want to know what works. Especially, they want to know what works for them. Their ideology and their value system are one and the same. The good, the true, and the beautiful is that which works for them.

On the surface, this situation seems to represent an impossible situation for the church. It means that each individual is only concerned for what works for him or her, rather than in universals. We cannot speak to this generation about rival ideologies and inconsistencies between worldviews and ever hope to get anywhere. On closer examination, however, a different picture appears. The tremendous power of ideologies over the minds of individuals has suddenly grown pale. We do not have to deal with the competing claims of a system. We only have to deal with the gospel's ability to provide meaning and purpose to life. We can be even more specific because we are dealing not with an idea but a person. We only have to deal with the ability of Jesus Christ to provide meaning and purpose to life.

Some will view this analysis as crass and crude for stressing what people might get out of a relationship with Jesus Christ. Surely, we ought to have purer motives for deciding to follow Jesus Christ. One of the most important theologians of all time took this position. Pelagius argued that people can clean themselves up. The church immediately recognized this view as a damnable heresy. The fact is that no one comes to Christ from pure motives, because no one has pure motives until Christ makes purity possible. Everyone comes to Christ through need. Perhaps Augustine expressed this experience best in his *Confessions* when he said, "Our hearts are restless till they find rest in thee."

IDENTITY

Third, ideology provides people with a sense of identity. The question of identity has a close relationship to the question of meaning, but identity asks, "Who am I?" This question also appears as one of the great developmental tasks of adolescence. People who lack a sense of identity lack self-confidence and the ability to relate well to other people in life. Ideology provides people with an identity by providing them with an easily understood label. Our identity is wrapped up in our ideology. Thus, he *is* a Democrat. She *is* a feminist. They *are* environmentalists. This feature of ideology does not mean that ideology represents the only way to label people and provide an instant identity. We label people many ways. Ideology, however, represents a way people can acquire a new label when they have outgrown the one that was imposed on them.

As we grow up, other people impose labels on us that identify us. We are identified as the child of Jim and Mary, the younger brother of Jack, the granddaughter of Bill and Susan. We are labeled in the education process by our intelligence (smart, stupid), our appearance (fat, slim), where we attended school (good school, bad school), and on the list might go. Ideology presents an opportunity for people to redefine themselves. In primitive times, a person was defined in terms of the relationship to the tribe. In modern times, ideology provides the new tribal identity. One should note that with the collapse of modernity and the rejection of ideology, in many areas of the world people have reverted to the old tribalism. We see this trend expressed most clearly in terms of which group is killing whom in the ethnic clashes around the globe.

The Christian understanding of creation and being made in the image of God has some important implications for the whole issue of identity. These basic understandings of what it means to be human involve the uniqueness of each person in terms of creation, yet the sense in which each individual has as a part of his or her identity a common relationship to one another and to God. By creation, we understand that we are made separate from God, but by virtue of our creation in the image of God, we share something in common with every other person and that common point has to do with God. Ideology does not touch the essence of a person and that person's essential identity, but creation in the image of God does touch the essence of a person. Thus, we can never truly know ourselves and have a true sense of personal identity without knowing the God in whose image we are made. We will always struggle to know who we are until we know in whose image we are made.

THE LOST AND FOUND DEPARTMENT

Though the postmodern generation seems to have rejected ideology and its metanarrative, it continues to struggle with the questions that ideology attempts to answer. Jesus Christ offers answers to these questions. The postmodern person is not so much interested in the ideological framework or institutional structure that Christians may present as being interested in knowing if Jesus Christ "works." Does he pass the pragmatic test.

Two thousand years ago, Jesus Christ addressed these same questions when he described what it means to be "lost." In fact, he described his mission in terms of seeking and saving that which was lost (Luke 19:10). Zacchaeus did not belong to the community. His identity had been defined in terms of his collaboration with the enemy. Jesus gave Zacchaeus a new identity by drawing him into the small community that centered around Jesus. Zacchaeus found the meaning to his life in terms of his relationship to Jesus.

Postmodern people will probably not become Christians by hearing that they can find meaning, identity, and community through Jesus Christ the same way Zacchaeus did. That sermon is to remind Christians that Jesus provides these things. Postmodern people become Christians by coming to know Christ the same way Zacchaeus did. He had heard enough about Jesus that he genuinely wanted to know much more. The final step in his conversion, however, was highly relational. He had heard the teachings of Jesus, but he had to experience the personal ministry of Jesus.

The greatest responsibility of followers of Christ in any generation involves carrying on the ministry of Jesus in such a way that people see Jesus through them. The three parables he told about what it means to be lost emphasize this fact. In this sense, Christ means for the church to be the lost-and-found department of planet Earth. Each of the three parables in Luke 15 ends with the community rejoicing together over what has been found. Something is lost when it is out of its intended context, when it cannot carry out its purpose because of separation from where it is meant to be.

The story of the lost sheep emphasizes that each individual has worth and meaning to God. Once again the issue of value, particularly the value of people, arises. People experience lostness in the sense that they feel something is missing in life. They often go off "in search of themselves." At the end of the Vietnam War, hoards of young Americans went off to Europe in search of themselves. I went too, though I went to see Europe. I reasoned that if I wasn't where I was, then I couldn't very well find myself where I wasn't. Yet, people spend their lives searching for the missing ingredient to make life worthwhile. Empires have been conquered and great fortunes acquired all to find the missing thing. Jesus suggests that we are what is missing. We are out of place in relation to the One who gives life meaning.

The story of the lost coin suggests that God feels the loss caused by our absence. For something to be lost, it must have value to the one who has the right of possession. For this reason, God experiences human loss even more than we do. These stories more than any other passages in the Bible help me understand why God came into the world. God cares about what is lost.

The story of the lost son suggests that all people must decide for themselves if they want their meaning and identity to be tied up with God. Some people change their minds in the course of life. The son did not make a pure decision to return to the father. He made a pragmatic decision. His survival depended upon it. In returning to the father, however, he becomes a part of an entire community that rejoices with the father. In fact, each of the three parables as well as the story of Zacchaeus ends the same way. A group of people rejoice with the one who has regained what had been lost. God is the loser when people are lost. The sad part of the story is that one person who had been hanging around the father all along did not care about what the father cared about. The elder son did not share the father's heart. The elder brother could not rejoice.

It is not hard to condemn postmodern people because they do not fit any of the acceptable Christian ideologies. They do not fit the mold. They go against the grain. They do not belong. It is not hard to love the old ideology more than the one for whom Christ died. It is not hard to confuse the old ideology for the old, old story of Jesus and his love. It is not hard to confuse the institution for the Savior. It is not hard to miss the point.

With the rejection of ideology, however, Christians have an opportunity to present someone who has the answers to life's perplexing questions. Nature abhors a vacuum. We should not assume that the apathy we call the rejection of ideology will continue as a characteristic of whatever the next great age will be. If Christians do not offer the clear option of Jesus Christ, people will find some new and terrible ideology.

PART THREE

PHILOSOPHICALLY CONFUSED

The emphasis on personal experience has awakened in people the awareness that they have the capacity to know things other than through their physical senses. Pluralism has forced an emotional retreat from rationalism, which tends to force people to make choices.

Reliance upon the senses and the scientific method created a world of absolute certainty during the modern age. Truth consisted in what could be proved empirically. Oddly enough, the modern world made statements about the transcendent that it could not observe, verify, or falsify; such as the psychological view that the idea of God is a projection onto the universe. Modernity could not recognize realities that lay outside its frame of reference. The philosophers described this situation by calling religious categories "non-sense" and by dismissing them with the aphorism, "Whereof we cannot speak, thereof we must be silent."

In the complexity of life created by modernity and in the failure of science to answer the profoundest questions, people turned toward a search for the transcendent with the opposite assumption from modernity: there is something out there that we cannot know through our senses. In this sense, postmodernity has much in common with premodernity. Virtually any metaphysic is open to consideration. Christianity offers a way to know the transcendent world, and as such the postmodern person will give it a fair hearing.

The postmodern generation does not require logical consistency. Rationalism was the twin sister of empiricism in the modern age. Christianity embraced rationalism with wanton abandon as it constructed highly rationalistic theological systems on the right and on the left. By buying into rationalism, Christianity accepted modernity's loathing of paradox. How can you have A equals A and A does not equal A at the same time? Modernity would also ask how Christ could be both human and divine.

The central truths of Christianity fall within the category of paradox, and they do not create the problem for the postmodern mind that they held for the modern mind. Scripture does not present faith in the kind of logical system that appeals to the rationalism of modernity, but it does present truth in the patterns that appeal to postmodernity.

CHAPTER SIX

THERE'S MORE TO LIFE THAN MEETS THE EYE: EMPIRICISM

Current scientific thought can be dangerous to faith. When religion poses explanations for natural phenomena, or things that occur in the physical world, and these explanations conflict with the explanations of science, then people of faith must make a decision to believe the explanation of science or the explanation of faith.

I have read the account written by a young man who was pursuing an academic career. He rejected his faith because of the teachings of science. The account is all the more startling because he took his faith quite seriously; he studied the Scriptures, and spoke about his faith with more mature believers. In the end, however, he rejected his faith because its teachings on the origin and nature of the cosmos conflicted with the latest scientific thought. Eventually, he would take up another religion that made more sense because of its consistency with his new scientific understanding.

The young man's name was Augustine. The religion he rejected was Manichaeism. The science he accepted was Ptolemy's view of an earth-centered universe. The religion he later embraced was Christianity. This all happened fifteen hundred years ago. The Manichaeans had adopted many terms from Christianity and had appropriated scriptural passages as well, but had given all a vastly different meaning. The differences appeared most graphically in their description of the relationship between the Father, Son, and Holy Spirit and the material world. The sun was called Christ and was worshiped. The moon was the dwelling of the wisdom of God, and the air was the dwelling of the Holy Spirit. The divine nature was mixed with the material substance of evil represented by people. As the divine part of the "elect" was released, it passed back to the sun and moon, which accounted for eclipses and changes in the appearance of the moon. The sun (Christ) was actually a triangular window through which the light of God shone on the world. Augustine accepted this view until he studied the mathematical calculations of Ptolemy, which allowed a person to predict with accuracy the movement of the heavenly bodies.

Though science led him to reject his religion, it did not provide him with a new understanding of what kind of God exists and how God relates to the physical world. He did not take Christianity seriously because it worshiped a physical God with hands, eyes, arms, and a face, according to the Bible. Though he had rejected Manichaeism, he still retained the deeply embedded Manichaean concepts and depiction of other religions. Not until he heard Ambrose of Milan preach did he come to understand the metaphorical and allegorical use of language in Scripture. Yet, he was still bound by a world-view that could not conceive of spiritual substance. His reading of Plato helped him understand how God could be spiritually substantive, have no aspect of evil, and create the physical world as a good thing. Augustine finally embraced Christianity as a faith that did not conflict with science. He became the guiding theologian of Christianity for one thousand years through the medieval period and, through his influence on Luther and Calvin, the guide for Protestantism.

THE PROBLEM OF SCIENCE AND RELIGION

Augustine's struggle demonstrates the problem of science and religion. It may be easy to see that the Manichaeans had misstated the cause of the movement of the heavenly bodies, but we also know that the current science of that day developed by Ptolemy also misstated the description of the operation of the heavenly bodies around the earth. One interpretation of the Bible seemed foolish to Augustine, yet another interpretation gripped his soul and changed his life. The person of science and the person of faith must both grapple with the problem of interpretation. In the case of Augustine, we see that he brought an entire set of assumptions to his initial interpretation of Scripture, which had become so much a part of him that he was not conscious of them.

Ptolemy and Copernicus interpreted the same data, yet they reached different conclusions. Copernicus concluded that the sun sat at the center of the heavenly bodies, instead of the earth. Galileo explored this idea experimentally with his telescope and came into conflict with the authorities for his views. Oddly, Galileo was not punished because his views conflicted with the Bible, but because his views conflicted with the prevailing philosophy of science based on the teachings of Aristotle. The academic establishment had so entwined their philosophy with their interpretation of the Bible that they could not recognize that they had imposed Aristotelian philosophy on the Bible.

This problem of the confusion of philosophy with one's science and faith can be seen most recently in Carl Sagan's famous words in introducing his television series. He declared that this is the cosmos and the cosmos is all there is. The statement is not a scientific statement derived from experimentation using the scientific method. Instead, it is a philosophical statement based on naturalism. Many people confuse naturalism with science and impose its views on the interpretation of scientific data.

THE PROBLEM OF MODERNITY

Thomas Aquinas invented the modern world in the thirteenth century, though he did not know he had done it. It would not become apparent for five hundred years. Aquinas changed the basic question people asked. The great theologian before Aquinas was Augustine who died about A.D. 430. Augustine had invented Christendom, the whole idea of feudalism, and the Middle Ages by asking the question, "What kind of God exists?" That was the basic question he needed answered before he became a Christian. He needed to know what kind of God exists. What he came to believe was that the kind of God who exists is a creator of the universe who rules over all the universe; who is sovereign over the affairs of all people, all places, and all times; and who has control of eternity from beginning to end. That is the kind of God that exists. The kind of society that developed in the Middle Ages mirrored that fact. There was a hierarchical system in which all authority derived its relationship from God.

In his conversion from paganism and his earlier understanding of what God is like, Augustine was helped along by Plato's philosophy. Plato's philosophy helped him come to an understanding of what reality is like before he ever took the Bible seriously. Thomas Aquinas was born into a world that assumed the existence of the Creator God, so Aquinas did not have to struggle with the same question. He lived in a culture that knew what kind of God existed. Aquinas asked "What can we know because God exists?" which is an entirely different kind of question.

Aquinas was fascinated by the philosophy of Aristotle. Aristotle had taught that when you come into the world, your mind is a blank slate. You know nothing to begin with, and all you will ever know is what you discover by observation. This view is known as *empiricism*, or the idea that real knowledge comes through sense experience. The only real knowledge comes through hearing, seeing, touching, tasting, and smelling. Thomas Aquinas used the philosophy of Aristotle to help him think about God. Aquinas said that the reason we can know anything is because God exists. God made real things, and we can know them by observing them.

Now that sounds fairly simple, but it was a radical idea in the world outside of the Christian West and the Muslim Middle East. Most of the people in the world at that time, meaning the people of the Hindu subcontinent of India and the continent of Asia including China and all of its tributary states, were either Hindus or Buddhists. They believed that, in fact, the world did not exist because there was no creator. It only seemed that there was a world here, so why bother to observe it? With his question Aquinas made science possible, modern science as we know it. Unlike Hinduism and Buddhism, he affirmed a real world that is substantial, and unlike Islam which also affirmed a real world, he affirmed the Incarnation. God came into this world and took on flesh, which means this world that he created matters to him; and therefore it should matter to us. The theology of Aquinas encouraged people to be involved in observation and learning because God cares about his creation. This perspective is the foundation for the modern world and for a scientific method. Western science comes out of Christian theology, but Christian theology in an Aristotelian Greek philosophical framework. That framework is very important. When people come to the Bible, they bring some kind of cultural presuppositions or philosophical worldview along with them.

Time passed and Galileo, the great Italian, invented the telescope and verified the theory of Copernicus about the motions of the heavenly bodies. Through his observations he concluded that the planets do not revolve around the earth. Instead, the earth and the other planets revolve around the sun. The earth is not the center of the universe. He got in trouble for that view. The way the story is often told is that he got in trouble with the church and Christianity and that Christianity persecuted him. Actually, Galileo got in trouble not with the church so much as with the academic establishment because he was disagreeing, not with the Bible, but with Aristotle. Aristotle and Ptolemy said that the earth was the center of the universe. Galileo went against the official academic position; and because the academy was a subdepartment of the church at that time, the church got drawn into it. But it was an academic dispute. As a result of Galileo's controversy, the importance of objective observation as the basis for knowledge and truth was only heightened. The emerging scientific method gained respectability as the true way of knowing, a superior way of knowing, even when it came in conflict with the official teachings of the church.

By the time of Isaac Newton, we see science moving beyond just the observation of facts to the construction of theories and laws about knowledge on the basis of the observation. Newton observed the motion of objects and proposed his laws of motion. For Newton, the discovery of laws was possible because God had established ordered patterns in the universe, and these patterns reflected God's design. For Newton there was absolutely no conflict with the Bible or belief in God. For him it was the wonder of having a glimpse of what God had done.

The practice of establishing laws of science based on observation began to move out into other fields. In the nineteenth century, we find the theory of evolution developing based on observations of various animal lifeforms encountered by Charles Darwin on a world cruise. We find Sigmund Freud developing theories about the identification of the cause of psychological disorders. This tendency to develop laws spread out into all kinds of other fields as people wanted to give more credibility to their discipline. I think the most ludicrous of these would be laws that are used in determining market timing in the stock market. Different market timers describe the laws they use to know when the market is going to go up and when it is going to go down. Market timing comes from this fascination that the modern age has had with trying to make a science out of what is often really an art.

Over the centuries from Aquinas to Einstein, bit by bit Christians embraced the scientific worldview of empirical knowledge. They embraced the idea of knowledge by observation or empiricism, because it really does sound like it has a theological basis. We can go to the Psalms and read

> The heavens declare the glory of God;
>   the skies proclaim the work of his hands.
> Day after day they pour forth speech;
>   night after night they display knowledge.
> There is no speech or language
>   where their voice is not heard.
> Their voice goes out into all the earth,
>   their words to the ends of the world. (Ps. 19:1-4)

With the Enlightenment of the 1700s in France, a slight shift occurred. God became unnecessary for knowledge, which was quite different from Newton's perspective. Science became the standard of knowledge. Scholars began to be aware in a new way that God could not be examined. How could God truly be known if God could not be examined by the "true" basis for acquiring knowledge? As we know from the old expression, "familiarity breeds contempt," as science became more familiar with creation, creation lost its wonder. There have really been very few true atheists in the world. Even in the scientific community, very few people actually embraced atheism. Mostly, people just began to live their lives increasingly oblivious to the presence of God. As the world ceased to be a mysterious place, everything could be explained. God may still be there, but he lives far off. The theory of God as a watchmaker, who may have made the world but wound it up like a clock, left it, and went off about his business, came to be popularly held.

During this period the church increasingly accepted the idea that scientific knowledge is the real knowledge. Both conservatives and liberals adopted this view, brought it into their theology, made it part of their methodology and their hermeneutic for studying the Bible. Beginning in the late eighteenth century and increasing into the nineteenth century, we saw a movement toward the scientific study of the Bible. This movement began in Germany with the schools of higher criticism, but it occurred in the United States with dispensationalism. The Scofield Study Bible was an attempt to arrive at the scientific understanding of the Bible. With Charles Finney, the American evangelist, we see the attempt to establish the Laws of Revival. Once determined, pastors could follow these procedures and have a revival in their church. In the twentieth century, we see the application of empiricism in the Church Growth Movement, which attempts to use scientific principles to establish the principles by which churches grow. This fascination with empiricism is not unique to liberals; it is something that the whole Western church has embraced in one way or another. Rudolf Bultmann, the German Greek scholar, accepted the presuppositions of science that include the idea that "dead men tell no tales." According to empiricism, Jesus could not have risen from the dead; but Bultmann wanted to create a place for faith without any specific content. His whole effort was aimed at providing a rationale to still have faith yet not have an Atonement, a Resurrection, or life after death. In the fundamentalist/modernists debate, both sides assumed an empirical worldview. The Bible must be accurate according to a scientific standard, so a scientific understanding of what is real became the standard for evaluating the Bible. Conservative apologetics and liberal theology sought to make Christianity acceptable to a scientific worldview.

THE PROBLEM OF POSTMODERNITY

Against the backdrop of an empirical tradition dating back to the Middle Ages, we find this new postmodern worldview gradually appearing in the twentieth century. Bit by bit the chinks began to appear in the armor of empiricism, but in the last ten or fifteen years this trend has begun to mushroom. The postmodern generation has rejected the absolute claim to knowledge that science enjoyed for so long. There is a growing scientific skepticism among the postmoderns that replaces the spiritual skepticism of the moderns. Now people accept the unexplainable. People believe in things that cannot be demonstrated. Dorothy Sayers, the English Christian apologist, was also a famous mystery writer during the thirties and forties. In *The Unpleasantness at the Balona Club*, her detective, Lord Peter Wimsey, complains that there is no hard and fast evidence to prove what he and everyone else knows. They know who did it, but they cannot prove it. The criminal that everyone knows to be guilty cannot be convicted for lack of adequate proof. The point she is making in that story is that we can know God exists but lack evidence to prove it scientifically. The postmodern person says that you do not have to prove it scientifically if you already know it. You see, it is a generation that now accepts multiple forms of knowledge as equally reliable, which is quite different from the modern era. People know now that there is more out there than meets the eye.

At the same time there is a growing distrust of scientific knowledge. We see this in such things as the Elvis Presley observations, this curious, curious phenomenon of people claiming to have seen Elvis, which is related to UFO observations. In 1996 in Arizona there was a big buzz about odd lights in the sky. There were newspaper reports about it. On national network news we saw home videos of a triangle-shaped object that flew over a town. Many observers believed it moved about thirty-five miles an hour and hovered about one hundred fifty feet above the ground. The science editor for this broadcast, however, placed little credence in the videotapes explaining that our faculties of observation are quite unreliable. The moon looks the size of a dime when we observe it in the sky. There has to be some way to correlate the meaning of the observation. The postmodern person is increasingly skeptical of the reliability of observation itself.

Postmodern people have grown up with science and technology such that it does not produce awe and wonder for them. Think of the changes in this century in communication: the telephone, the radio, the television, the VCR and other recording equipment to augment the broadcast equipment, the computer, the Internet to connect computers, the World Wide Web to make the connection more graphic and visual, and the development of virtual technology. The advances are explosive. Little children five and six years old have absolutely no wonder and awe and amazement about things even though older adults are flabbergasted with every new development. We see the same advances in transportation. To think that we began this century with the marvel of heavier-than-air flight going over a hundred feet in a bamboo and silk aeroplane, but we end it with no one even bothering to watch liftoffs anymore from Cape Kennedy. The problems with the Mir Space Station are dealt with the way we deal with an old automobile. Let's just get a new one. The postmodern generation has no sense of wonder and awe. They see new discoveries proving old discoveries wrong. So they say you just never know. They are now in the same position that their ancestors were two hundred years ago—familiarity breeds contempt. There is nothing special about the technology. They know that sensory knowledge is flawed and that verifiability may work, but only within certain limits.

The cultural shift taking place in the West that has been called post-modernity is having a curious impact on science. Many scientists are searching for an acceptable "spirituality." Carl Sagan is dead. The naturalistic philosophy of modernity adds nothing to the scientific data, yet it adds nothing to personal life either. Eastern religions have become more popular because they allow a person to develop a form of spirituality, yet without a content that might conflict with the scientific data.

Christianity seems to have little to offer because its content appears to conflict so dramatically with the scientific data, even if it does offer a rich source of spirituality. Some scientific people resolve the problem by living in two worlds in an uneasy truce. The problem grew to such a barrier in the modern period because the church bought into the scientific worldview so completely in the nineteenth and twentieth centuries. Scientific truth was the most respectable truth; therefore, the truth of Christianity must be scientific truth. Scientific truth must be concrete, measurable data; therefore, the Bible must be literally true or not true at all. Thus, Christianity in the West split into two camps, with a third group of noncombatants uncomfortable with the extreme positions.

Liberal theologians like Rudolf Bultmann accepted the assumptions of secular science in his interpretation of the Bible. He reasoned that because dead men do not rise from the grave, there must be some other explanation for the resurrection accounts in the Gospels. Fundamentalist theologians, on the other hand, rejected the leading theories of modern science because they conflicted with a literal reading of the first chapter of Genesis.

Thus, the philosophical assumptions of modern liberalism and fundamentalism became barriers to faith. Liberalism drained Christianity of its transcendence, and fundamentalism drained it of its connection with the physical world of experience.

THE UNCERTAINTY PRINCIPLE

The scientific method created a false sense of security in terms of what people can know for certain. Confidence in the reliability of objective empirical observation led to what has proved to be an unwarranted sense of certainty about what we can know. From the time of Isaac Newton until the revolutionary insights of Albert Einstein, this confidence prevailed not only in the scientific world but also in the popular imagination.

Albert Einstein helped destroy the notion of scientific certainty in the first decade of this century when he came up with the simple little formula $E = mc^2$. He declared that space was curved rather than flat. The shortest distance between two points was not a straight line as everyone had known since the time of Euclid. Instead, Einstein reasoned that in the vast expanses of space, the shortest distance between two points might be a curve. Time and space were relative matters and only the speed of light was constant. Such matters affected the outcome of observations depending on one's location and what one was observing. Though he shook the notion of certainty, the initial impact of the breakthrough was only understood by a handful of scientists. The implications of Einstein's theory of relativity would take almost a century to work their way through the scientific community to the other academic disciplines and finally to the popular culture.

Einstein's work in 1905 effectively destroyed Newton's universe. Einstein changed the way scientists think about the universe. In opening up this empirical can of worms, however, he also demonstrated how our philosophical prejudices make it difficult to grasp an idea that clashes with our preconceived notions. At the time of his work, most scientists believed in a static, unchanging, everlasting universe that had no beginning. The equations that Einstein developed to explain relativity, however, would not support a static universe. Rather than give up the prevailing view of the universe, Einstein added into his calculations what he called the *cosmological constant*, which offset the implications of his own theory.

Einstein's special theory of relativity had some intriguing implications for empirical observations. Relativity proposes that time passes at a different rate for a stationary observer than for a moving observer. If two people are stationary, their watches will tell the same time; but if one of them is moving around the world in an airplane or to the moon in a space shuttle, when the two people come back together, their watches will tell different times. This discrepancy grows with the speed and distance at which objects move. In his foreword to the truly postmodern book *The Physics of "Star Trek,"* Stephen Hawking comments on how enormous the discrepancy can grow: "If the *Enterprise* were restricted to flying just under the speed of light, it might seem to the crew that the round trip to the center of the galaxy took only a few years, but 80,000 years would have elapsed on Earth before the spaceship's return."[1]

When Einstein conceived of relativity, space flight existed only in the mind of Jules Verne. In fact, heavier-than-air flight had only been achieved two years earlier by the Wright brothers. Einstein relied upon a much slower but common travel experience to illustrate the discrepancy of observations.

Imagine someone traveling on a train who has set up an experiment to measure the distance and speed of a pulse of light from a bulb on the ceiling to a mirror on the floor and back to the ceiling. The observer on the train will observe the light traveling in a straight line, the shortest distance between the floor and ceiling. The light travels at 186,000 miles per second. A second observer outside watching the train pass by will observe something different. The trackside observer will see the man, bulb, and mirror moving sideways. From this perspective, the light will have to travel farther because the mirror has moved as the light pulse approaches it, and the ceiling has moved as the light pulse is reflected back toward its source. Bird hunters understand this concept. Instead of shooting straight at a bird flying across a hunter's field of vision, the hunter will "lead" the bird and shoot ahead of it so that pellets and bird arrive at the same spot at the same time. By aiming straight at the bird, the bird will have passed by the time the pellets reach the spot where the bird had been when the episode began. Because light always travels at the same speed, the person outside the train will observe that the incident took longer because the light had farther to travel. Einstein concluded that time is not a universal that is standard in all places. Instead, it is quite personal and local.

Relativity also had implications for the observation of space. Using the train example again, we can see how motion affects the observation of physical objects. If an observer on the train measured the time it took for a light pulse to travel the length of a train car, the observer could calculate the length of the car, because the speed of light is constant throughout the universe. The outside observer would calculate a different length for the car, however, because of the motion of the car. If the light source faces the rear of the car, the forward motion of the car will mean that the light has a shorter distance to travel because the rear of the car is rushing forward to meet the pulse of light. If the light source faces the front of the car, the forward motion of the car will mean that the light has a farther distance to travel because the front of the car is rushing away from the light. The effect for the outside observer will be that the train car appears to be longer or shorter than the observations of the person inside the moving train car.[2] Einstein reasoned that as objects approach the speed of light, space collapses to near zero and time stretches to infinity.

Einstein's special theory of relativity did not challenge the validity of empirical observation, but it did shatter some of the fundamental assumptions about the nature of the universe in which empirical observations are made. It also introduced the idea that observations may be "relative." The special theory of relativity brought the first serious challenge to the idea of Absolutes though it only specifically challenged the idea of Absolute Rest and Absolute Time. Einstein destroyed the mechanical universe of Newton, but with it the Moral Absolutes of the deists could also be challenged by analogy. Maybe morality was "relative" as well.

The second, and perhaps greater challenge to certainty, also came in the early days of the twentieth century. While Einstein's theories of relativity deal with explanations of the universe at large, quantum theory focuses on the tiny world within an atom. Max Planck used the term *quanta* to name the tiny-sized packets in which he reasoned light must come. Einstein received the Nobel prize in 1921 for a paper he wrote, which argued that Planck's quanta would explain the photoelectric effect, or why some metals give off electrons when light strikes them. As quantum theory developed, however, it took some turns that Einstein found more disturbing than other scientists had found his relativity theories.

Before quantum theory, scientists thought of the atom as a tiny solar system with particles traveling around a nucleus the way planets travel around the sun. The developed physical models of the atom that looked like billiard balls or Tinkertoys with little sticks connecting them. All of this conceptualization gave a solid appearance to the atom, which seemed to give the universe a solid foundation. Quantum theory changed all that.

Quantum mechanics explores the strange world of subatomic particles. This field of science has created a crisis for all of science because it has destroyed the old absolute certainty associated with an older philosophy of science. Instead of moving around the nucleus like a planet around the sun, electrons "jump" or "leap" from one location to another around the nucleus. During this quantum leap, the electron moves from one position to another, but it does not travel. It is as though it ceases to exist in one spot and suddenly appears at another spot, like Jesus when he went from the meal in Emmaus to a room in Jerusalem. As physicists examined electrons, they discovered that they could locate the position of an electron or the velocity of an electron, but they could not determine location and velocity at the same time. Furthermore, they determined that electrons possessed mutually exclusive and contradictory properties. Electrons behave like particles (fixed, discrete points) and waves (continuous extensions). In order to measure these subatomic particles, it is necessary to use a quanta of light. These tiny packets seem insignificant to us; but to the particle being measured, it is the same as being hit by an automobile. In other words, the attempt to measure accurately creates an inaccurate measurement.

One of the marks of modern science had been its confidence in the deterministic nature of the universe. To know the position and velocity of something means one can know the past and the future of that object. Quantum theory changed all that. One could only predict with probability the future behavior of objects. Werner Heisenberg formulated this feature of quantum theory as the *uncertainty principle* in 1926.

After several centuries of expecting science to provide all the answers, physicists now doubt the certainty of observations. The very act of observation distorts the data being observed at the subatomic level, and the contradictory nature of the subatomic world has led a growing group of physicists to doubt the reality of the physical world. The data is neutral, but the interpretation of the data introduces an ever-growing collection of philosophical biases. Eastern religions provide an attractive way to make sense of a world that no longer fits the old philosophy of science. In Hinduism and Buddhism we do not have a "real" world. The physical universe is either an illusion or a delusion.

Christianity offers another attractive understanding that allows people to continue to believe in an objective physical world. While we affirm an objective universe, we believe that the all-present, all-powerful, all-knowing, immortal God who created it took on flesh in a particular body in a particular time and place, and then died on a cross. The affirmation of the Incarnation of God in Jesus Christ has stood at odds with the same tradition of logic that blinks in the face of quantum mechanics. But if such a God exists, it would not be surprising to find at its fundamental level that the universe reflects the nature of God. The sublime behavior of electrons reflects the full deity and full humanity of Christ.

Finally, chaos theory combined with quantum theory gives a one-two punch to the old deterministic model of a closed universe. The average person can identify with chaos theory best each evening when we watch the weather report knowing that the poor souls forecasting the weather miss it as often as not. In the secure closed environment of a controlled laboratory experiment, a scientist can predict with great accuracy the result from introducing changes in barometric pressure, temperature, humidity, and wind velocity. In the real world, however, the variables multiply at an incalculable rate. The laws of physics still work, but in the context of a wide-open system that has been dubbed "chaotic." One need no longer do logical gymnastics to make a case for the intervention of God into the old closed universe of Newton. Instead, chaos theory suggests that the universe is not closed at all, but wide open for God to interact with creation from the subatomic to the cosmic levels. Rather than thinking of the intervention of God and the suspension of the laws of nature, chaos theory suggests an open universe in which God has freedom of expression.

CONCLUSION

Where does that leave the church, the Christian faith, and the gospel? I think it creates a tremendous opportunity because the good news in communicating faith to postmodern people no longer has to deal with the apologetic issue of making the case for the possibility of the knowledge of things that cannot be seen. That is, we no longer have to make a case for the spiritual world. Now, revelation is as valid a way of knowing as is sensory experience. Postmodern people accept the idea of holy writings. They do not see the Bible as having any exclusive place, but they accept it as a way of knowing something. We do not have to make a case for it anymore, nor do we need to feel that it requires some sort of scientific explanation. They are a pragmatic people. They want to know if it works.

The effective engagement of the world with the gospel of Jesus Christ in the future will require Christians to examine seriously their own philosophical presuppositions about their faith and about science. We cannot expect non-Christians to bear the responsibility of making sense of our faith. As a result of the discoveries of quantum mechanics, modern science has been thrown into a crisis about what science can know with certainty. Uncertainty is not such a bad thing in scientific or religious speculation. It forces us to slow down and be a bit more humble in our declarations.

Augustine became a Christian when he discovered that some parts of the Bible speak allegorically and metaphorically about the spiritual truth of how God relates to the world. Relieved of the old scientific theory of knowledge, Christians may once again explore how God creates and relates to the world. The scientific theories that our old philosophical assumptions tell us to fear most and fight with all our vigor may be the very opening that makes sense of faith to the skeptic.

For most of the twentieth century, both liberal and conservative Christians created a barrier to the hearing of the gospel by scientifically informed people. By accepting the mechanical model of the universe or naturalistic philosophy, liberal theologians drained Christianity of its transcendence. By assuming a literal meaning to the opening chapter of Genesis, conservative theologians imposed a theory of science necessary to salvation. As we move into a new century, perhaps we can learn an old lesson from Augustine. If our message is tied too closely to any particular theory of science, then when new scientific theories come, our message will be discarded with the old science. On the other hand, if our message cannot transcend the shifts in science from a flat earth sitting on four pillars, to the earth-centered world of Ptolemy, to the sun-centered solar system of Copernicus, to the mechanical universe of Newton, to the relative universe of Einstein, then perhaps we have misunderstood the message of the Bible. As Christians consider their responsibility to make Jesus Christ known to people who long to make sense of their world, we will do everyone a service by reflecting on how our habitual ways of dealing with biblical faith and science may need revision.

CHAPTER SEVEN

CONSISTENCY IS THE HOBGOBLIN OF SMALL MINDS: RATIONALISM

By the time of the split in the Christian church in 1054 between Eastern Orthodoxy and Roman Catholicism, the East and the West thought about God in entirely different ways. Their process or mode of thinking and talking about God differed. They believed in the same God revealed in the Scriptures, but the way they expressed their theology differed. In the Eastern church it was mystical. In the Western church it was scholastic.

In the eleventh century Anselm of Canterbury wrote his major book that set a tone for theology in the West, *Cur Deus Homo?* or *Why the God-Man?* In this book, he explored why God had to come in the flesh. Anselm also constructed a famous argument for the existence of God. He followed a rationalistic approach of one proposition requiring acceptance that builds a case to prove a point. His argument may be restated as:

1. I have in my mind the idea of a most perfect being than which no greater can be conceived
2. But a being that actually exists would be greater than one which only exists in my mind
3. Therefore, God exists.

This rationalistic approach worked well in the Middle Ages because the medieval mind read the argument with the fundamental presupposition, "Of course God exists." The "proof" did not so much prove the existence of God as it demonstrated how Western theologians thought about the existence of God.

During the Middle Ages, the scholastic movement grew and flourished. The Schoolmen developed the art of argument and reason with such questions as "How many angels can dance on the head of a pin?" and that question would keep them going for months and months. For almost a thousand years the theology of Augustine guided the Western church. Augustine, in turn, had been influenced by the philosophy of Plato. During the high Middle Ages Western theologians rediscovered the philosophy of Aristotle, which encouraged debate between those who thought like Plato and those who thought like Aristotle. The ancient philosophers provided a logical framework for developing systematic theology. Thomas Aquinas would follow Aristotle in developing a new way of thinking about God.

In the Reformation, John Calvin went with Augustine, who was Platonic in his thought and advocated categories of prior knowledge that people are born with. The scientific world, on the other hand, went with Aquinas and Aristotle and the idea that our minds are a blank slate without any universal or archetypal ideas. The division between rational, scholastic, and academic versus the emotional, experiential, and spiritual, came to characterize Western thought by the time of Descartes. This growing separation forced people to choose to think scholastically, rationally, coldly, and methodically or to think more experientially, emotionally, and related to the mystical and spiritual. Descartes, who was in a dilemma about whether or not he existed and questioned the reliability of observation, finally resolved the problem rationally. Sitting in an oven until he could come up with a solution, he popped out of the oven, completely baked, with the statement, *"Cogito ergo sum,"* "I think, therefore I am." This episode, as much as anything, helped solidify rationalism as the governing mode of thought for Western white males, because they were the ones who went to school and wrote the books.

You had to be a Western white male to be a monk. Remember that the uniform of the academicians is still the monk's attire: the robe and the hood. Academic professors are still referred to in terms of ecclesiastical degrees. "Bachelor" was a monastic title, and all the academies were monasteries. The master of the academy, the master of the monastery, had charge of all the bachelors. Those who achieved great learning were called "doctors," which is "teacher," or more precisely, teacher of doctrine. Of course, only the boys went to school. The girls made lace in the convents. The embrace of rationalism produced a certain way of thinking. My wife has suggested to me that men and women think differently. Into modern times there has been a male control of the means of communication, learning, politics, and religion. As a result, rationalism has been the official "real way to think."

Christians fell in love with the modern world's love of rationalism. Both conservative and liberal theology developed highly rationalistic systems. Systematic theology, unlike the theology of the Eastern Church, is highly rationalistic. Reformed theology of conservative Calvinists is every bit as rationalistic as the liberal theology of German rationalists. In England, deism considered a personal, involved God who acted in the world as irrational. The deists replaced the personal and involved God with moral laws.

Rationalism produced an approach to theology that is logical and orderly, and if things do not fit within the system, you leave them out. Rationalism attacked and undermined Christianity in the modern world because it could not tolerate Christian ideas that seemed to contradict rational logic, such as the Incarnation and the Trinity. How can something be fully God and fully man at the same time? How can God be three persons in one? It doesn't work. How do you deal with human freedom and Divine sovereignty? In certain kinds of logical systems, you cannot deal with such issues satisfactorily. Arminianism opted for human freedom while Calvinism opted for Divine sovereignty. Such issues cannot be dealt with by the kind of rationalistic system that has prevailed during the modern era. So philosophy rejected metaphysical or spiritual ideas as "nonsense." Something is nonsense if you cannot know it through the senses. Religious words were viewed as having some meaning, of course, but only meaning to those who are involved in the group. They had no "real" meaning, as referring to an external object. When Christians say "God," it represents a comforting concept; but the word does not refer to an objective reality. The linguistic philosophers would allow religious people to use religious language, just as long as they understood that it did not mean anything except to religious people. This development presented a very paternalistic, patronizing view.

THE POSTMODERN REJECTION OF RATIONALISM

With this prevailing approach to logic and rationalism in the Western world, the postmodern generation rejected the modern world's devotion to rationalism. They rejected the idea of "right thinking" with the "right" kind of logic. In terms of their international exposure, they have learned that there are many ways to think around the world. There are other systems of logic, other processes for making sense of the world, not just one. Logic operates like a language. In fact, at many universities students can receive credit toward their foreign language requirement by taking a logic course instead of taking a French or a Spanish course. Computers have different kinds of languages. At Union University the computer that operates our library system uses a UNIX language system. The computer that sits on my desk uses an MS DOS language system or logic system. All people in the world have a language, but they do not all speak English. All people in the world have some kind of logical system they use to make sense of the world in which they live, but they do not necessarily have a Western white male rationalistic system. The postmodern generation has said, "Well, that may be logic to you; but that doesn't mean it's necessarily the only way to think about it."

The tradition of Western rationalism is a linear way of thinking—like a recipe or like a math equation. The postmodern generation has a preference for other kinds of logic, for instance, narrative thinking, like a story. This approach is not just postmodern, it is premodern. Preliterate societies have a preference for a narrative way of thinking. This preference is both premodern and postmodern, it is preliterate and postliterate. One might think of an emerging postliterate society. A postmodern preference for thinking includes patterns and relationships. Such thinking would be more like a collage as an art form than an architect's plan. The experimental education TV program for preschoolers *Sesame Street* uses quick cuts and unrelated sequences to teach an approach to processing information quite unlike anything that has gone on before in Western civilization.

MTV uses this same way of processing information. It uses these flash points, but a look in the New Testament at the Sermon on the Mount reveals the same approach. In the Sermon on the Mount Jesus takes an idea here, an idea here, and an idea there, all woven together to make a point. New Testament scholars of the twentieth century have tended to reject the idea that the Sermon on the Mount represents a single presentation by Jesus Christ. Why? The reason given is that it does not reflect Western linear scholastic thinking. It does, however, reflect the kind of thought processes and logical systems of first-century Palestine. Whereas higher critical Christian scholarship embraced rationalism, the postmodern world has rejected it, with the scathing critique that the modern person does not admit or recognize the prejudices or presuppositions that determine what the outcome is going to be before you even start the process.

All thought systems are based on prior presuppositions and values. Something is built into the system. We think this way. Thought processes are not purely objective. This is the postmodern view, though Paul, Augustine, and Calvin might agree. There is something flawed about all of them, but logic is how we interpret and give meaning to data.

So where does that leave us? Is it scary? A little bit, because I admit I have been trained as a modern thinker; it is my habit, though I am also aware of the fact that I've been showing signs of this postmodern organizational system lately. Preachers have a strong ability to move in that direction if a sermon is not ready by Saturday night. You grab things here and you grab things there and you just hope. Maybe it will make sense. On the positive side, however, in communicating faith to the postmodern person, religious language is no longer regarded as nonsense. In fact, postmodern people view religious language as quite important. Postmodern people are interested in religion, but they have no background. They are true first century pagans, and religion is all like a cafeteria. Take what you want. But the good thing is, they are open and approachable. Religion represents another way of understanding the world, so let me hear about it. The postmoderns are like the Athenians who said to Paul, "Well, tell us more." After the materialism of modernity, religion poses not just interest, but fascination. "Tell us a new thing." They will give religion a hearing; but in rejecting the old rationalism and the old scholasticism, they are also saying, "Don't give me a lecture. I will talk with you, but don't give me a lecture."

The message of the gospel may be unveiled in a conversation; but traditionally, in the twentieth century, evangelism and personal witnessing have been a lecture on how the vicarious substitutionary atonement works. It is not a conversation like Jesus had with the woman at the well. It is not a conversation like Jesus had with Nicodemus. It is not the kind of thing we see going on between Jesus and people. Recent witnessing presentations are a linear presentation; and when we get to the end, you'll be saved. This approach is like going into a classroom and hearing a lecture. Postmodern people do not want that, but they will talk.

As uncomfortable as the rejection of rationalism may be for most Christians who value the intellectual dimension of faith, this rejection removes a significant barrier to faith. It is no longer necessary to "prove" the existence of God. With their suspicion of rationalistic logic and philosophical argumentation, postmodern people have a preference for intuition and ways of knowing that lie outside the boundaries of official modern knowledge.

Postmodern people recognize the relationship between rationalism and rationalization. They have grown up cynically recognizing the word games of TV commercials. Rationalism and other forms of argumentation have all the appearance of a trick. It sounds like a sales pitch. When people of faith use the language of rationalism, they sound like "peddlers of the gospel," which Paul warned against (2 Cor. 2:17). People will talk freely about spiritual matters, but they will cut off a lecture or a sales pitch.

Modern Christian philosophers frequently appeal to the "Law of Non-contradiction" to prove that postmodern people do not think correctly and to persuade them to change the way they think. Unfortunately, this argument tends to be self-defeating because it appeals to an assumption they do not accept. Noncontradiction is not a law of nature handed down by God. Rather, it is a rule of the game of logic practiced in the West. It is not a rule of logic practiced in the East.

Oddly, the "Law of Noncontradiction" has been a cudgel with which modernity has flailed away at Christianity for centuries. The question of *Why the God-Man?* was not settled by Anselm nine hundred years ago. He merely acknowledged the logical contradiction of the central article of the Christian faith. The philosophical speculations on the relationship between the Father and the Son spawned one heresy after another until the final settlement of the issue with the Nicene Creed. Only, the creed did not stop the philosophical attempts to resolve the contradiction of God and Man being one but separate. The doctrine of the Trinity only adds to the problem.

Postmodern people have a high tolerance for contradiction. The Incarnation does not by itself repel them. They may not believe it, yet at the same time they do not deny that it may be true. In other words, they do not have a built-in resistance to the gospel because it offends their sense of logic. This suspension of judgment creates a climate that permits conversation about something rare and extraordinary that does not correspond to any other experience of life.

Though postmodern people reject rationalism, they have not rejected rationality. People must have some basis for rationality in order to function. The rationality of postmodern people looks different from the rationality of modern people. Rationalism operates like a chain. It is strong, and each link fits in a determined sequence. The links all follow the same, predictable connection. With the postmodern person, however, the connections are less predictable. Instead of a strong, sequential chain, the rationality of a postmodern person more closely resembles the relational database of a computer. While thinking about one thing, bits of data spring together into a pattern that makes sense. When thinking about something else, other bits of data are brought together. Nothing is neat. The problem for the postmodern person is having a "program" that works to help them organize the data. The gospel offers such a program to help people arrange the data of their lives into patterns that make sense. In this way, noncontradiction may come to the postmodern person, but it will come as a conclusion to faith in Christ rather than as a prerequisite for faith in Christ.

The Bible itself has no apparent rationalistic organizational scheme. It does not fit into the neat categories of a book on systematic theology in which topics are pursued in a logical and sequential manner. Yet, the Bible reflects a rational understanding of reality. The connection between individual books written over a period of a thousand years in different cultural settings does not rely upon a rationalistic system to make sense. Instead of delivering ultimate truth in philosophical syllogisms, the prophets of Israel spoke in poetry. Whereas the modern church labored to translate the Bible into rationalistic theology to make it more acceptable to the modern person, the Bible represents the kind of information montage to which postmodern people respond.

The difference between modern thinking and postmodern thinking can be seen in how one deals with repentance and faith. The modern person desires to know the proper sequence of repentance and faith in the order of salvation. The postmodern person, on the other hand, desires to know the relationship between repentance and faith in the experience of salvation. During the development of rationalistic faith during the late–Middle Ages, theology came to be called "The Queen of the Sciences." Oddly, the Bible says nothing of theology. Instead, it speaks of meditation. Theology is not a science. Rather, it involves meditation on one's own experience with God in light of the revelation of Scripture. While the modern person prefers the objective detachment of theology as a scholarly pursuit, the postmodern person prefers the experience of God as the necessary basis for theology.

Anyone who has followed the voyages of the star ship *Enterprise* has witnessed the shift in attitude concerning rationalism as a new generation has come of age. In the original *Star Trek* episodes, Mr. Spock embodied pure logic. Captain James Kirk embodied emotion. The characters represent the polarities and dichotomies that rationalism presented to the modern mind. One had the choice of being logical or emotional. In *Star Trek: The Next Generation* the dichotomy disappears. The captain tempers judgment with compassion. The counselor who advises the captain on critical decisions relies on empathy, rather than logic for guidance.

Postmodern people have no intention of going back to rationalism. Christian scholastics who want them to return to the old philosophical framework have committed the error of confusing rationalism for the Christian worldview. Western Christianity, both Catholic and Protestant, so embraced rationalism for so long that it came to be identified with the faith. But it was only the wineskin. It provided a package for the faith.

THE POWER OF STORY

People love stories.[1] No matter where they live in the world, no matter if they are rich or poor, people love stories. Americans sit in front of the television set to drink in the story on the tube. Tribal people sit around the fire at night as the old people tell the stories. Many times my daughters have climbed up in my lap when they were little and asked, "Daddy, will you tell me a story?"

With all of the technological advance of the modern period, perhaps the most dramatic inventions have been used to perpetuate the ancient need for stories. While the modern person developed an analytical culture that glorified objective fact and emotional detachment, the thirst for stories increased. The political and economic treatises of the English Renaissance continue to be read by a handful of scholars; but every school child knows the stories of Shakespeare, which continue to be produced and read. The great analytical works of the nineteenth century have achieved "classic" status and are required reading for Ph.D. candidates, but people in everyday life still read Dickens.

Moreover, the great stories continue to be produced in media accessible in every home. Leaders of government and education saw the development of the radio as a means of stimulating and educating the population, but the people wanted to be entertained. Radio delivered laughs, music, and sports; but most of all it became a focus of storytelling. Television brought entertainment to the visual level. People could see the games and the singers; but most important, they could see the story taking place. The variety show has all but disappeared from television, but prime time still focuses on telling stories. Sitcoms, soap operas, detective stories, and westerns represent a few of the major types of stories told on TV. They represent different approaches to stories.

In the last twenty years a new kind of storytelling has grown to dominate a major segment of the air waves. Americans watch talk shows in huge numbers. This new form of storytelling is the oldest form of storytelling. It simply involves people telling their own story. Americans crave stories, especially real stories. Thus, Americans watch programs devoted to showing amateur home videos in the same numbers as watch professionally produced programs that cost millions of dollars to make. People listen to Oprah Winfrey and her imitators by the millions. They listen to accounts of real life. Do they listen for answers or rationalizations of their own situation? Do they listen out of boredom or loneliness because they do not have a significant personal connection in their own life? Listening to stories of the lives of other people helps us survive. From ancient times, the biography has remained a standard and popular form of literature.

Shortly after the New Hampshire primary of 2000 in which Senator John McCain upset Governor George W. Bush in their race for the Republican nomination, columnist and political commentator Robert Novak spoke at my university. Novak is a rationalist in the grand old tradition who believes in a critically thoughtful political philosophy. In explaining why the people voted for McCain, however, Novak insisted that it was because McCain had a story. The power of the story of a prisoner of war who refused the opportunity to go home without his comrades overshadowed considerations of political issues.

By adopting rationalism so completely, Western Christianity virtually abandoned half of what it means to be human. The creative, artistic, emotional, experiential, personal, relational, interior dimension of life easily becomes lost in a highly rationalistic world. The Christian faith gave birth to the cultural art forms of the West. Music, drama, literature, and art all flowed from the Christian understanding of life, creation, order, beauty, and truth. As the modern age dawned, however, Christianity and artistic expression became seemingly opposites. The Protestant Reformation identified wholeheartedly with the new rationalism while Catholicism clung to the preservation of old forms and traditions. Both streams of Christianity in the West ceased to use the arts as contemporary expressions of faith.

Christians have not had a significant impact on art in the West since the eighteenth century. The Catholic tradition has accepted the dichotomy of sacred art and secular art, while the Protestant tradition has ignored art as irrelevant or counterproductive to the gospel. During this period, the proclamation of the gospel has become identified with rationalism. The Puritans in England in the early seventeenth century referred to their preaching missions as "lectureships." It has become fashionable in recent years to blame everything bad in American Christianity on Charles Finney while yearning for a return to the days of Jonathan Edwards. Many Christian writers blame Finney for all the subjectivism in religion today as well as all the concern for pragmatic methods. At the same time they look to Edwards for intellectual credibility. This caricature of the situation ignores Edwards's concern for experience and Finney's extreme rationalism, seen in his cataloging of the "laws of revival."

Attempts in recent years to establish a beachhead in the world of art seem wooden. Christian production companies produce Christian movies, which depend upon a cognitive explanation of how the substitutionary atonement works in order to give the movie validity. By straining to insert a lecture in the Puritan tradition, the movie abandons what it most powerfully does. The art forms of a culture set the tone for a culture. They establish, define, defend, and promote the values of the culture. When Christianity abandoned the art forms, it abandoned the culture.

In the face of the general rejection of the art forms, some Christians have continued to express themselves in the arts in spite of the lack of support, and often in the face of criticism. G. K. Chesterton succeeded in troubling the young atheist C. S. Lewis. Lewis, in turn, would discover that his fiction had the power to reach into the hearts of people. Lewis would live his life as that thing he grew to despise most: a modern man, in the sense that he always retained a bit of the rationalist that had been drummed into him by his education. Yet, he also recovered that ancient spiritual power of the story known to all cultures. His apologetics could operate on the rationalistic level with his masterpiece, *Mere Christianity*. He could communicate just as powerfully, however, in two other nonrationalistic forms. At the artistic level he wrote *The Screwtape Letters*, *The Chronicles of Narnia*, and his space trilogy. At the personal, testimonial level, he wrote *Surprised by Joy* and *A Grief Observed*.

For most of the twentieth century, Christians have imposed a rationalistic understanding on 1 Corinthians 1:21: "It pleased God by the foolishness of preaching to save them that believe" (KJV). Preaching has meant the delivery of a sermon to the modern church from the time of the Puritans who taught that preaching was "the ordinary mean and instrument of the salvation of mankind."[2] While the preaching ministry remains essential to the worshiping, gathered body of believers, this form of communication is not necessarily the most effective in reaching and influencing the shape of contemporary culture. The sermon and the speech were the spiritual and political means available for influencing public opinion two thousand years ago. At the beginning of the twentieth century, Teddy Roosevelt made much over the "bully pulpit" as a way to sway the masses. By the time his cousin Franklin became president thirty years later, however, the world had dramatically changed. While FDR could deliver a good speech, he influenced the public with "chats" over the radio. He was a media personality like Jack Benny or Bing Crosby.

While many preachers have taken to the air waves, very few have learned to adapt the style of communication to the medium. For most, radio and television serve to broadcast the sermon. The 700 Club and the PTL Club represent two highly successful and notable exceptions to the normal use of broadcasting by Christians. Unfortunately, the PTL experiment ended in scandalous disaster. The 700 Club has managed to attract a loyal following of Christians, but its primary focus has been on galvanizing a loyal corps of Christian followers who will do battle against the culture rather than trying to shape or influence that culture.

While Christians ignored the artistic dimension of mass communication to concentrate on the rationalistic, the entertainment side of television and radio shaped American values. The shape of family values and social norms came from *All in the Family*. Archie Bunker represented everything a right-thinking, feeling person did not want to be. He made every position he espoused seem ridiculous. He opposed premarital sex, abortion, and homosexuality. These positions were linked with racism, bigotry, and exceptional ignorance. Of course, Archie was a Christian and a hypocrite.

The movie industry promoted the sexual revolution of the 1960s with such trend-setting movies as *The Graduate* and *Goodbye, Columbus*. On television *MASH* and *Maude* made fun of every traditional value that undergirded the culture. Ministers were portrayed as clowns or crooks. Devout Christians were portrayed as mean, meddling hypocrites. No counter voice was heard because Christians had withdrawn from the primary stage that forms public opinion. They had retreated to the rationalistic media of sermon and speech.

While the road back to serious cultural engagement is a long one, Christians can take clues from the leading cultural icons as they seek to help individuals encounter Jesus Christ. The television programs that survive for more than one season scratch an itch that the viewers feel. Several programs that have little artistic merit have lasted for years. *Cheers* had the same plot on every episode. The characters continually repeated their character flaws: sexual addiction, alienation, low self-esteem, loneliness, inability for intimacy and commitment. *Cheers* could just as easily have been called *Church* because of the tremendous needs of the people involved, and the theme song could easily be sung as a contemporary Christian chorus:

> Sometimes you want to go. . . .
> You want to be where everybody knows your name.[3]

Critics complained that *Seinfeld* was not about anything. It had the same plot each episode as well. It involved an even smaller group of friends who were preoccupied with sex, but who wanted meaningful personal relationships. Now the popular show simply says it: *Friends*. The Neilson ratings will tell us the most pressing spiritual issues in America today. Average Christians may not have access to a TV production company, but they can talk with their friends about what bothers them.

When Jesus taught, he did not deliver long, boring lectures. He told stories that we call parables. He knew that something about a story makes people stop and listen. Cultural critics complain about the phenomenon of Americans who appear to be "glued" to their television sets. The critics seem to forget that the need to hear stories did not arise in America. Samuel Taylor Coleridge based one of the greatest poems ever written in the English language on the power of story. In "The Rime of the Ancient Mariner" (1798) he tells of an old sailor who stops a wedding guest just outside the church. The guest is next of kin to the bridegroom and must hurry in, so he asks why the old sailor has stopped him. The old sailor simply replied, "There was a ship." With those words, the old man had the guest in his power. Once the story had begun, the guest had to hear it out. The guest can hear the music in the church. He later hears the gaiety of the reception. Finally, all have left except the guest and the old sailor who finishes his long story.

The power of a testimony lies in the fact that it tells a story. When Christians give their testimony, they tell their own story. The testimony has many advantages as a way of communicating the message of the gospel in a way people are willing to hear:

Unique—No two people have the same testimony. That makes everyone's testimony special. The uniqueness of a testimony keeps it from boring people.

Identifiable—Despite the uniqueness of a testimony, people can identify with another person's experience. All people share the same basic needs and emotions. A testimony helps people see the similarities of their own life with which they can identify. If Christ could help the one sharing the testimony, perhaps he will help the one who identifies with it. A testimony helps people see themselves clearly. What we could never admit about ourselves suddenly becomes clear when someone else says it about themselves.

Interesting—A testimony creates interest in the same way that gossip draws attention. A testimony contains the drama of life. It might not be dramatic in the sense of Paul's experience on the Damascus road, but any story that comes from the heart has true drama.

Relevant—A testimony demonstrates that the gospel of Jesus Christ still has meaning two thousand years after the Resurrection. In a personal testimony the contemporary truth of the gospel shows itself. A testimony reveals what Jesus Christ means to someone on a day-to-day basis.

Personal—Unlike some methods of evangelism that rely on a canned approach, a testimony has a personal edge. The testimony comes from the heart of the person who shares it. They did not learn it from someone else.

Authoritative—The very nature of a testimony gives it authority. Because a testimony tells what we know of our own experience, no one can deny it. They may not believe it, but they cannot deny it. We are the final authority about what Christ has done for us.

TELLING YOUR STORY

Every Christian has a testimony. The testimony does not have to tell of a life of crime dramatically transformed. A testimony tells of how Christ has saved someone and how he has continued to make life worthwhile. Glittering testimonies may have excitement, but most people will not identify with them. Most people do not lead glittering, exciting lives. The testimony of an ordinary person has particular power because most people are ordinary.

C. S. Lewis had one of the most powerful testimonies of any Christian in the twentieth century. He wrote his testimony in an autobiography called *Surprised by Joy*. Literally thousands of people came to Christ as a result of this testimony and the other writings of Lewis. Lewis had a dramatic testimony, but not a glittering, exciting testimony. Lewis lived an ordinary, some would say dull, life. He taught medieval English literature at Oxford. He never learned to drive. He lived most of his life as a bachelor. But he had a powerful testimony about how Jesus Christ saved him.

Ordinary people pose a greater challenge in witnessing than very bad people. Very bad people know how bad they are, and in their heart they know how far from God they stand. Ordinary people, on the other hand, consider themselves pretty good. They tend to believe that if there is a heaven, they deserve to go there. For these ordinary people, an ordinary testimony has particular power. If someone like them discovered their need for Christ, then maybe they need him too.

A testimony tells how Christ saved us, but it also tells what Christ has meant to us since salvation. We only have one testimony of how Christ saved us. We have hundreds of testimonies of what he has meant to us. Part of the testimony involves remembering what he has done. In a sense, a testimony is a thanksgiving time when we acknowledge what he has done for us. In another sense, a testimony is a bragging time when we want someone else to know how great our Lord is and why we love him so.

THE RATIONALITY OF STORIES

When we tell our testimony, several points need to come out. Like any good novel or movie, the testimony needs development. It also has to have enough detail that it does not sound like a general experience that could have happened to anyone. Yet it should not have so much detail that it sounds tedious and boring. A good testimony will usually, but not always, have four points:

1. **Introduction**—Set the stage in the introduction. Give some background to your experience with Christ. In a conversion testimony, describe your life before you became a Christian. In a testimony about how Christ has helped you in life, describe your situation before the crisis developed in which you needed help.

2. **Crisis**—The drama builds as you describe how a crisis grew in your life. In a conversion testimony, describe how you realized that you needed

to be saved. In a testimony about how Christ has helped you, describe the crisis that led you to lean on the Lord.

3. **Climax**—The critical moment of the testimony comes with the climax. God does something. In a testimony, the Lord is always the hero who rescues us. In a conversion testimony, describe how the Lord saved you. Did someone lead you to him? Did it happen during a revival? How did you feel? How did you turn to him? In a testimony about how he has helped you, describe what he did about the problem that you faced. How did you know the Lord had helped you? Did you ask him for help?

4. **Resolution**—The resolution tells what life has been like as a result of what the Lord did. In a conversion testimony, tell what difference the Lord has made in your life. In a testimony about what the Lord has done for you, tell how salvation means something every day. Describe what it means to know the Lord loves you and cares for you, even when you do not ask.

PART FOUR

THEOLOGICALLY IGNORANT

The postmodern generation does not have a theological position so much as it lacks a theological position. It has not rejected Christianity, because it is generally unaware of the Christian faith.

Modernists could not separate their opinion, system, or ideology from "truth," therefore the postmodernist has concluded there is no truth. Modernity was an age of ideological "isms" and scientific hubris. Eastern thought has always operated from a different system of logic while the West confused a logical system with the truth.

Postmodernists are usually characterized as not believing in ultimate truth when in fact, they are searching for the ultimate truth. For Christians, this search opens unparalleled opportunities for presenting the gospel. The challenge for Christians, however, lies in their own capacity to distinguish between their theological system and the ultimate truth of the gospel. This chapter will argue that all theology is wrong, though some is more wrong than others. Theology is meditation about God, though during the modern age the church has made theology a science.

Modern liberal and evangelical theology became respectable by intellectualizing the spiritual domain out of theology. The spiritual was left to Pentecostals and Catholics who had the common decency to "do it" according to a tradition that could be rationalized in the modern world as aesthetic. People with a postmodern orientation have no difficulty with the supernatural in the Bible; but unlike most contemporary Christians, they also have no difficulty with the supernatural occurring today.

A plethora of explanations and speculations about the spirit world are available today. The church has an opportunity to interpret this reality to a pagan world in a way it has not had since Patrick landed on the shores of Ireland fifteen hundred years ago. People are now prepared to accept spiritual reality. The question remains whether or not the church will be prepared to talk about such things.

No country, culture, society, or civilization has ever lasted. God has judged them all and found them lacking. The prophets of Israel described this process in detail, yet God's people continue to cling to the romantic notion that their country or culture or society or civilization is just what God had in mind. At the Ascension the disciples were still asking if the kingdom was about to be restored to Israel, but Israel's time was past. The book of Revelation describes the final judgment of nations and cultures and individual hearts. The success of the gospel does not depend upon the continuation of modernity any more than the success of God depended on the continuation of Israel. In each age and place, however, God opens a door through which the gospel can pass. It keeps the church from growing lazy. And it reminds us that "we have this treasure in earthen vessels."

CHAPTER EIGHT

FEELING GOOD WAS GOOD ENOUGH FOR ME: TRUTH AND VALUES

In the movie *Return of the Jedi*, Luke Skywalker complains that his teacher, Obi Wan Kenobi, lied to him. Obi Wan had said that Luke's father had been killed by Darth Vader, when actually Darth Vader *was* Luke's father. This was a dramatic moment in that movie. To this accusation of lying, Obi Wan Kenobi replied that when the father was seduced by the dark side of the Force, then he ceased to be himself. Obi Wan argued that it was true that Darth Vader killed Atticus Skywalker—at least, "from a certain point of view."

The postmodern generation does not believe in the truth as an absolute thing. Everything is relative; it all depends upon one's point of view. Something may seem true from one certain point of view and false from another certain point of view, but nothing is "true" or "false" in and of itself. The modern world had made dramatic claims about what is true and what is false. Especially was this so in the realm of science. Truth came to be regarded the same as the scientific method. Real truth consisted in what a person could verify through experimentation, observation, and duplication.

As the modern age rolled along and we moved out of an age of kings and monarchies to an age of other kinds of political systems, political movements started making these equally dramatic claims about what constitutes truth. We saw Communism making dramatic claims about the truth, and fascism making equally dramatic and contradictory claims about the truth. From time to time even democracy has made dramatic claims about what is truth! Philosophically, the truth meant the philosophical system that a person uses.

Now, philosophers are not just people who live in ivory towers somewhere, and say obtuse and convoluted things. Everybody is a philosopher, because philosophy is simply a matter of how people think, and we all think. Everybody has a philosophy, and they express it in simple terms. "Seeing is believing" represents an entire philosophical system. This philosophy of knowledge is called *empiricism*. People with this philosophy of knowledge do not believe what they cannot experience firsthand. Doubting Thomas followed that kind of philosophy: "Unless I see the nail marks in his hands and put my finger where the nails were, and put my hand into his side, I will not believe it" (John 20:25*b*).

"If it ain't broke, don't fix it" represents another approach to philosophy called *pragmatism*. This approach does not waste time worrying about what we can know. This approach is only concerned with what works. In this concern with what works, people do not really care about value and morals and ethics; it's just a matter of "does it work?" If it works, it is good. If it does not work, it is bad. Oftentimes even Christians have gotten into this business of understanding truth in which we have relied on a philosophical approach. Christians have tended to see the truth as the theological system they have accepted or the philosophical system behind their theological system. It might be neoorthodoxy; it might be Calvinism; it might be Arminianism; it might be dispensationalism. These are all philosophical systems for interpreting Scripture, and people have a tendency to regard their system as the truth. Because we use a philosophical system for interpreting Scripture, we tend to confuse our way of thinking with God's revelation.

The confusion of philosophy and revelation happens because we tend to confuse logic with the truth. In the West we have come to equate Western logic with what is really true. But all over the world there are many different kinds of logic. Logic is only a matter of how we make sense of the world. It operates like language. Everybody has a language, but not everybody speaks English. Everybody has a system of logic, but not necessarily our system. For this reason, in the modern world truth came to mean nothing more than individual preference.

MODERNITY'S TAKE ON TRUTH

The dramatic advance of science accelerated steadily from Newton to Einstein and then exponentially during the twentieth century. Alongside this advance the philosophy of *naturalism* developed until it exercised a major influence on the modern world. According to naturalism, all phenomena may be explained according to natural forces. Stated more extremely, nothing exists that may not be explained by natural forces or processes. When Napoleon asked Laplace where God fit into his theories, Laplace replied, "I have no need of that hypothesis." Naturalism has no place for God, but naturalism also has no place for absolute truth or absolute values.

Newton assumed the existence of God, even though his view did not fit classical Christianity. He adopted a view of God that kept God at arm's length from nature. God set everything in motion, including all the "laws" Newton set about to discover, then he withdrew from creation. In addition to the physical laws God established, Newton and most scientists and philosophers of his age believed that God had also established moral laws. This view of God, which swept through the scientific, theological, and intellectual communities of the West during the eighteenth century, is known as *deism*. Deism provided a philosophical basis for separating God from nature and morality. Truth, in turn, became an aspect of science in terms of nature and of philosophy in terms of morality.

This fragmentation of knowledge into specialized disciplines led to the tendency to think of truth in terms of the discipline itself. As we saw in chapter 3, fragmentation results in a loss of the whole. While the whole is greater than the sum of its parts, concentration on the parts results in the loss of that which is greater. The focus on the individual parts in science resulted in the loss of the need for understanding the relationship of the parts to each other. The separation of the questions of the scientific method from the questions of the philosophical method meant that each realm of knowledge could thrive without having to consider broader issues that relate to the whole.

Philosophers like Descartes, Pascal, and Newton had to consider both the physical and nonphysical realms. The development of deism, however, allowed for the great divide of the disciplines. In the nineteenth century this divide became permanent when the natural philosophers adopted the new term *science* to describe their discipline. Descartes had helped this process along in the 1600s by making popular the idea of a mind/body dualism. It took two hundred years to work itself out, but by the 1800s this dualism had separated those who studied the mind and spirit (philosophers) from those who studied the body and matter (scientists).

Without the need to consider ultimate spiritual matters, Charles Darwin was free to suggest a theory of evolution that could be explained entirely by natural processes. In fact, without the option of considering ultimate matter beyond the physical, a scientist has no choice but to attempt to explain all phenomena exclusively by natural processes. This trend in science took a dramatic step further away from the consideration of ultimate matters when Sigmund Freud applied the implications of natural selection to the study of the mind. The mind had belonged to philosophy, but Freud made it an object of science. Freud provided a theory based on naturalism to account for all of the high and lofty ideas of humanity, as well as for all of the low and currish ideas.

If the presence of humanity can be explained in terms of survival of the fittest, then the values of individuals can be explained in terms of survival mechanisms. One of the aims of psychology has been to free people from the bondage of absolute ideas like God or truth, which are seen as only wish projections. Likewise, Social Darwinism applied the implications of Darwin's theory to society as a whole. Growing into the discipline of sociology, this field accounts for group behavior in terms of survival and the exercise of power without recourse to any value or absolute that lies outside the group. Values are created that advance the survival of the group. The truth is nothing more than what the group values.

While the hard sciences (physics, biology, chemistry) and the soft sciences (psychology, sociology, anthropology) moved more and more in the direction of giving physical or natural explanations for what were spiritual matters, philosophy moved increasingly away from the physical world and even spiritual considerations. With Immanuel Kant in the early nineteenth century, the distant God of deism disappeared as an impersonal force remained. Kant was concerned with the moral question of what one "ought" to do, but "oughtness" as a force seemed rather weak. Hegel's dialectic provided a way of thinking of the force at work that drives history toward its conclusion. Marx built his great system on Hegel's dialectic and placed materialism at its center. Philosophy became increasingly stressed to account for truth or moral absolutes in a mechanistic, naturalistic universe.

The *existentialist* philosophers following Søren Kierkegaard focused their attention on the individual's quest for authentic existence in a world where people easily become lost in the crowd. The dilemmas of meaninglessness, lack of identity, and mortality provide the context in which authentic existence may emerge. An atheistic form of existentialism became popular after World War II in France following two dreadful wars and the collapse of the French overseas empire. Since nothing seemed to matter, existentialism provided thoughtful, despairing people with a way to make sense of their individual existence in a world that seemed futile. Existentialism in a Christian context developed in Germany during the rise of nazism. Rudolf Bultmann accepted the basic views of naturalism and concluded that there is no life except the one we live between the cradle and the grave. What matters is that we live a faithful life while we are here.

By the 1930s the great philosophical tradition of the West had collapsed into the individualism of existentialism and the irrelevancy of *linguistic analysis.* Ludwig Wittgenstein argued that language works like a game. Every group or *family of life* in society has its own way of using language and has its own meaning for the words it uses. Football players have one way of using language, carpenters another, and Sunday school teachers yet another. The meanings of words is determined by their usage, not by any objective reality behind the word. The word *God* has meaning to the Sunday school teacher, but it has no objective meaning. This trend in philosophy reduces all ideas such as truth, beauty, goodness, and God to mere social constructs. They have no independent existence from the group that uses them.

In the realm of Christian theology the fragmentation also took place, which called the idea of truth into question. Theologians of both a liberal and conservative stripe attempted to adapt the methodology of science with its expectation of absolute certainty. Higher criticism, comparative religion, and the quest for the historical Jesus represent areas in which theology attempted to treat religion in a naturalistic way. Dispensationalism and the laws of revival school attempted to discover the key to the interpretation of the Bible and the laws by which revivals operate. Both approaches tend to drain the transcendence from religion and make it something over which people have gained power to control and explain. Under the influence of Darwinian evolution, classical nineteenth century liberal Protestant theology embraced a view of the progressive perfection of society.

Karl Barth proposed an alternative to the old liberalism when the carnage of World War I suggested that people and society were not getting better and better. Barth wanted to recover the affirmations of the historic orthodox faith, but he also felt the need to affirm a naturalistic world. *Neoorthodoxy* became yet another way of expressing Descartes' mind/body dichotomy. The physical world can give us no ultimate knowledge of God. Barth rejected *natural theology* as a valid enterprise. On the other hand, he rejected the idea that the Bible represented specific revelation from God. The Bible contained a record of revelatory experiences with God that people had long ago. Barth believed that the revelation of Christ represented the ultimate revelation of God to people.

Neoorthodoxy became extremely influential in American Protestant Christianity. The de-emphasis of the Bible as revelation, however, led to the common expression of such phrases as "it became truth for me." A subjective dimension entered mainstream Christianity that gave the Bible a relativistic character. Christ may be the ultimate revelation of God, but what we know of Christ comes as statements in the Bible. These statements are not objective truth but represent the faith of the person or community that experienced Christ.

In the United States, neoorthodoxy presented an attractive alternative to fundamentalism for people who wanted to hold to traditional affirmations of faith without the dogmatic turn. Developed in German-speaking Europe after World War I as a counter measure to liberal theology, neoorthodoxy flourished in the United States after World War II as a counter measure to fundamentalism. In a strange way, neoorthodoxy prepared the way for the postmodern attitude toward truth and ultimate matters. For decades, the mainline pulpits proclaimed that the Bible was a collection of stories of faith but was not revelation from God. Only personal encounter with God is revelatory, and such an encounter is inexpressible. Therefore, the Bible should not be regarded as truth but as testimony by people who had spiritual experiences.

In the 1960s as people became increasingly aware of other religious traditions through the experimentation of the counterculture, the Bible became just one of many holy books in the world. It made no difference that neoorthodoxy claimed Christ as the ultimate revelation. It had no basis for the claim since its holy book was just a collection of spiritual experiences. The Bible and Christianity had no basis for making truth claims compared to other religions in the neoorthodox scheme. As a result, mainline American Christianity was unprepared to deal with the changing theological landscape. Neoorthodoxy provided answers to questions Europeans were asking in 1918, but it verified the postmodern conjecture that all values and truth claims were personal matters.

THE PURSUIT OF HAPPINESS

This approach to truth during the modern era gives us a clue to begin to understand what is going on with the postmodern generation. They looked at the modern world system and decided, "Well, that's just a bunch of hooey; there must not be any truth, if everybody is saying 'this is true, and that's true, and something else is true.' They all contradict, and it's just people arguing among themselves." So they have rejected the idea of absolute truth. Notice, they have not rejected Christianity, or God, because they have never known either one. They have never heard what the New Testament means by truth.

Every person has values. Every society has values. Values represent little more than what is important. Ebenezer Scrooge had values. One of these was revived by the postmodern generation during the beginning of the stock market boom in the 1980s as "greed is good." The Vandals smashed, burned, and destroyed the fruit of a thousand years of classical culture because the buildings and art of ancient Rome were not important to them. The name of that ancient tribe has been given to anyone who senselessly destroys something of value to someone else.

In this regard, the postmodern generation is regarded by many as a tribe of vandals at the gates of Western civilization on the verge of a great destructive rampage. To the extent that they do not value the great tradition of Western thought, they have the potential to be vandals. Oddly, the modern age produced far more acts of cultural vandalism than the postmodern generation will likely commit. The postmodern generation is largely ignorant of the great tradition of Western thought. They would not have encountered it at home, at school, or through the popular media. They never went to church, so they would be ignorant of biblical teaching. But they do have a deeply rooted value in the American tradition, though they are the first generation to embrace it so completely without other competing values.

Thomas Jefferson had the best of intentions, and on the whole, he did a commendable job of expressing the grievances of the colonies and declaring an alternative vision for what a society could be. Had his colleagues in the Continental Congress not pressured him to finish the memorial to the king, had the committee not pestered him with so many helpful suggestions, and had Philadelphia not been so insufferably hot that summer, Jefferson might have realized what he had said in time to correct it. He probably only included the last phrase in order to balance the first two ideas. None can argue with the fact that it sounds more stirring from a propaganda point of view to have the last phrase included: "life, liberty, and the pursuit of happiness."

With everything else that was going on that summer of 1776, Jefferson probably did not have time to reflect on what that last phrase meant. Doubtless, he had never intended to lay the philosophical foundation for the disintegration of that little nation he hoped to help start. Nonetheless, he created a time bomb. For most of this nation's history, the people of the United States had to devote all of their energy to the preservation of life and liberty without much time left over for even contemplating how to go about pursuing happiness. With my generation, however, we finally found the time.

We always had the privileged few who devoted all of their energy to pursuing happiness. Mr. Jefferson did his share; but for most of us, securing life and liberty required our total attention. We did not work for fulfillment and meaning; we worked to have food and shelter. As late as the 1960s and the Civil Rights movement, liberty remained a crucial issue that left little time to ponder how one would even go about pursuing happiness. With my generation, however, the pursuit of happiness emerged as a mass movement that replaced earlier concerns for the preservation of life and liberty.

It all began innocuously enough. The warning signs appeared in the late-1950s for anyone willing to see them. Who could miss the hula hoop! In a matter of months, every child in the country had a hula hoop. I remember hearing the parents of my friends talk about hula hoops. Of course the things were silly, but during the Depression they had to do without. The Depression generation wanted their children to have the things that they could not have had as children. And if a hula hoop would make them happy, what harm was there in buying one? Hula hoops were fun for a week or so before they got boring, but they did not make us happy. Since happiness did not lie in hula hoops, we began pursuing it elsewhere; and we have not stopped.

Everyone came up with his or her own list of what would make for happiness. As we grew older the lists changed. Beer, dope, sex, cars, and clothes were fun; but they did not make us happy. They just made us want more beer, more dope, more sex, more cars, and more clothes. Then we tried to modify the list when we decided only a certain variety of things would make us happy. We wanted the right friends, the right clothes, the right job, the right house in the right neighborhood, and the right sex partner. We learned that we could discard people as easily as hula hoops if they did not make us happy. We succeeded in turning all of creation inside out with each of us individually at its center judging the value of everything else in terms of its happiness value to us.

Pursuing happiness takes a lot of energy and does not leave much time for less fulfilling activity like caring for the homeless, finding a solution to the environmental crisis, tutoring inner-city children, neighborhood development, providing emotional support for fragmenting families, visiting the elderly, or simply spending time with one's own family. Pursuing happiness requires the total commitment of one's life energies. Pursuing happiness requires a dedication to a relentless, all-consuming quest that takes us from jobbing to cocaine to high fiber to TA to TM to channeling to mutual funds. Others become a means to our end, and happiness gets lost somewhere as the failed quest settles for isolated moments of pleasure. As Kris Kristofferson wrote and sang to us of Bobbie McGee:

> Freedom's just another word for nothin' left to lose. . . .
> Feelin' good was good enough for me.

A year after the Persian Gulf War, the experience of the Kurds and their struggle for life and liberty serves to remind us that the pursuit of happiness is a pretty shabby goal.

Of course the irony of this tragic little episode in the collapse of civilization is that my generation will never know happiness until it learns that happiness cannot be pursued. Happiness is not an ornament that may be acquired; nor is it an accident of one's circumstances, captive to the ebb and flow of fortune. Happiness is a gift. It cannot be squeezed from life. It is the by-product, the fringe benefit, of living for others rather than for ourselves. Without that, we lose the life and liberty Mr. Jefferson and his friends were really concerned to protect. Maybe after conspicuously consuming our way through the self-indulgent 1980s and 1990s, and finding nothing that satisfies, people will begin to look for something else.

Of the baby boom generation, those born between 1946 and 1963, 75 percent had a significant church experience growing up—at least two years in church as children or teenagers. Baby busters, those born between 1963 and 1977, flip-flopped the statistic. Only 25 percent had any church experience growing up.[1]

Consider the generation that began in 1977, that is now entering their twenties. We have them in our colleges and our high schools. They know nothing about the Bible, Christianity, or Jesus. When my little girl was two years old she knew about Moses in the bulrushes, David and Goliath, Noah and the ark, Jonah and the whale, Daniel and the lions' den. Notice how the Bible stories all come in pairs. She has known all the stories of the Bible from earliest childhood. Most young people in the United States today do not know who Jesus is. So they have not rejected the absolute truth of the gospel, because they have never heard it. They have rejected what the modern world meant by the truth, which is just a fashionable way of thinking until a new fad comes along. Oddly enough, what the postmodern person is really looking for, what postmoderns really want, is the stability, the rock, the anchor, the foundation, of the truth that they can stake their lives on; because they recognize the sham of the modern worldview that has been passed off as the truth.

What opportunity do Christians have for reaching this postmodern generation? How do we deal with this generation that is intent on sweeping away the past? Will we insist that they adopt the thought patterns of the philosophical system of the modern era, or will we tell them about Jesus? Jesus told his disciples "I am the way and the truth and the life. No one comes to the Father except through me" (John 14:6). We can either introduce people to the Savior and exalt him; or we can tell them about a theological system, and we can confuse our faith with our cultural preferences.

I'm suggesting the old cliché, that we get "back to the Bible." Unfortunately, this phrase usually means to return to an old theological system. Amazingly, both conservatives and liberals can drift away from the Bible as we get wrapped up in our systems. Virtually all of Protestantism came about as a product of the modern age. Most of the Protestant groups produced a great theologian, but Baptists never did. Southern Baptists in particular have violated the rules of Western theology by affirming ideas that do not fit consistently with how theologians in the West do theology. For instance, they affirm both "Once saved, always saved," and "Whosoever will may come." Now the first, "Once saved, always saved," is Calvinism. The second, "Whosoever will may come," is Arminianism. The Presbyterians, who are Calvinists, and the Methodists, who are Arminian, have told the Baptists throughout the modern era, "You can't believe both those ideas because they are not logically consistent." And Baptists have replied, "We can believe it, because the Bible says it." It may not be logical, but it is truth. The unlettered Baptist saw something higher than a system.

All theology is wrong. Some theology is more wrong than other theology, but all theology is human reflection about God. It is a human attempt to understand and talk about God. The Bible, on the other hand, is revelation from God. Which is more trustworthy? Theology will pass away. All the theologies of the past have passed away sooner or later; then we recycle them, dress them up, and start them over again. They may be helpful, but theology is not truth. God's word is truth.

OVERCOMING OBSTACLES

This issue of the relativizing of truth and values bothered me more than any other aspect of postmodernity. Every other aspect of postmodernity seemed to offer some door through which the gospel could pass. Since postmodernity deals with the rejection of modernity and modernity dealt with the rejection of Christianity, postmodernity cleared the field of so many modern presuppositions that stood against Christianity. The rejection of absolute truth and absolute values, on the other hand, seemed to offer no open door. Instead, it seemed to be a closed door that was heavily barred. In fact, none of the other possible doors seemed to matter if this one was closed.

The existence of absolutes has been a foundational concept of Western civilization since the time of Plato and Aristotle. Christian theology since the time of Augustine has depended upon an understanding of these universals. Catholics and Protestants have both utilized this kind of framework. When the deists were hard at work developing their moral law apart from the presence of God, they looked to these universals. The universals served people well. They gave people a basis for developing ideologies that had no need for God.

I wanted desperately to defend the universals because they form such an important part of my tradition. Unfortunately, they play no part at all in biblical revelation. They are a pagan idea. The universals stand alongside God or the gods. The universals provide a basis for judging God; and thus, they stand over God. The ancient Greek philosophers asked questions about "truth." They wanted to understand "the good." For them, these terms represented philosophical concepts. They were organizing principles that do not necessarily exist perfectly in the physical world. Things in the physical world may either reflect the universals or contain a certain degree of the universal, but the universal itself exists in another realm. The physical world may either point to the universal or be only a shadow of the universal; therefore, the universals remain a matter of speculation that no one can quite know.

The Bible certainly speaks of truth, goodness, beauty, and a number of other matters that we generally think of as pertaining to these universals. To these universals, we could also add such concepts as the value of human life and other moral absolutes. In the Bible, however, these matters are not self-existent truths or realities. They depend upon something else for their existence. They depend upon God.

If anything exists independently of God, then the God of the Bible is not the kind of God that exists. Twenty-five years ago when I first went to seminary, it was popular among *avant garde* ethicists to speak of the moral standards to which even God is subject. That line of thought bothered me then because it meant that something stood over God as judge. It meant that God submitted to some higher authority outside himself. The idea of universals, no matter how helpful they may be to erecting the moral society of Plato or the deists, involves *dualism*. It means that God has a rival authority. This view has had a tremendous influence on Western conceptualization of values. For the deists, it meant we could follow the rival authority and dispense with the necessity for God. The modern world could produce very moral atheists who followed the standards of the universals. The universals, in turn, became the standard for evaluating a person's right to immortality. Once again, God need not play any part in the journey from this world to the next.

The teachings in the Bible about goodness, righteousness, truth, and other matters considered by Christians as absolute are actually personal views. In this case, however, they represent the personal views of God. These concepts have no life of their own apart from God, just as my opinions have no life of their own apart from me. Of course, as the opinions of God, they have had quite a life! The opinions of God about his creation should have a higher standing than the opinions of a crew of bystanders like the human race. Yet, as creatures made in the image of God, we have the ability and the privilege of forming opinions of our own which differ from those of God.

The literal meaning of the Greek word translated *repentance* in the New Testament has the notion of changing one's mind. Many theologians and Bible students do not think this idea is strong enough. The concept of penance grew up to give us something extra to do because changing our minds does not seem significant enough. I might facetiously observe that of the theologians I have known, I cannot recall any that had much experience at changing their minds; so I am not sure that they realize how very difficult it is. To repent involves exchanging our view for God's view; trading our values for God's values.

The discussion so far has focused on what might be called positive absolutes, but the same would hold for negative absolutes as well. Evil as a self-existent, independent thing does not really exist. Evil represents the complete disregard for the values of God. Whether thoughts or actions, evil represents a personal rejection of God or what is important to God. Evil describes the totality of thoughts or actions that result from such a complete disregard for God.

Not all religious views would hold to this understanding of evil. In the dualistic religion of ancient Persia, Good and Evil represent eternal self-existing and equal forces. In the yin and the yang of the Tao of China, opposites represent two sides of the same reality. Good and Evil are two aspects of one universal. No such dualism appears in the Bible. Evil poses no challenge to God in the Bible. It is not his equal. It is not a rival. It only exists as a by-product of the attitude of personal beings to God. This does not so much mean that the postmodern generation is right as it means that the modern age was wrong. Some things are right and some things are wrong, but not because of universals. Something is universally wrong because of God's judgment of it.

We see this understanding of truth and values in the earliest passages of the Bible in terms of God's valuation of creation. As God saw the results of his creative activity, he called each aspect of it "good." This does not mean that he appealed to the universal category of good to describe his work. It means that what God does provides the criteria for determining "the good." Goodness is defined in the Bible in relationship to God, not to a universal idea. Jesus mentioned this understanding of goodness when he was approached by a young leader who wanted to know how to be included in the Kingdom of God. Both Matthew and Mark record the encounter. They focus on different aspects of the exchange, but they both intersect at this point about goodness as it relates to God.

Matthew focuses on the issue of *doing* good: "Now a man came up to Jesus and asked, 'Teacher, what good thing must I do to get eternal life?' 'Why do you ask me about what is good?' Jesus replied. 'There is only One who is good. If you want to enter life, obey the commandments' " (Matt. 19:16-17).

Mark focuses on the issue of *being* good: "As Jesus started on his way, a man ran up to him and fell on his knees before him. 'Good teacher,' he asked, 'what must I do to inherit eternal life?' 'Why do you call me good?' Jesus answered. 'No one is good—except God alone' " (Mark 10:17-18).

God and God alone is the standard for understanding goodness. The Good, which so perplexed the Greek philosophers is not a universal concept, a principle, or a force, as little children learn to pray "God is good. . . ." The postmodern generation has come to the point that it rejects the notion of universal principles, but they have not yet come to the realization that goodness, truth, and other values that have absolute authority derive that authority from their unique status as the judgments of God. At this point they are satisfied to say that everything is relative. Their sense of absolutes went the way of Newton's universe with its absolute science and absolute moral laws. In Einstein's universe, as we observed in chapter 6, everything is relative. Or is it? In terms of human observations of phenomena, everything is relative. Everyone has his or her own perspective that affects how one sees things. To say that everything is relative, however, is to say that things are relative to a standard. In the case of the physical universe, things are relative to the constant speed of light.

In terms of human experience, we all have the tendency to view qualities of truth, goodness, beauty, evil, and other intangibles from a rather limited perspective that centers around us. We bias our own values to suit ourselves. In this sense, the postmodern person rightly says that all values are relative. It is simply another way of saying that "the heart is deceitful above all things" (Jer. 17:9). Put another way by precocious little Anna in the tale of the little London orphan during World War II, people have a point of view, but Mister God only has points to view.[2]

The postmodern generation is not interested in grand philosophical explanations. They are up close and personal. They have rejected ideologies and absolutes, yet they still have to deal with truth and lies, beauty and ugliness every day of their lives. In many ways C. S. Lewis had an easier time of it than the postmodern generation. His thought crystallized on these issues during the period 1939 to 1945. During these years he wrote *A Preface to Paradise Lost*, *The Problem of Pain*, *The Screwtape Letters*, the collection that would become *Mere Christianity*, *Perelandra*, *The Abolition of Man*, *That Hideous Strength*, and *The Great Divorce*. This great body of work represents his most important work as a Christian apologist. Of course, Lewis had the advantage of Hitler in helping him recognize truth, goodness, and evil. It is much easier to recognize what is meant by evil and wickedness when one is on the receiving end. It is much easier to recognize beauty in the midst of ugliness. Truth, goodness, and beauty exist where the grace of God abounds. Where the grace of God does not abound, we find deceit, evil, and ugliness. It is much easier to deal with this issue when things stand in such stark contrast as black and white. The postmodern generation lives in a gray world. Black and white have been so mixed together that people cannot tell the difference until they are the victims of something they do not like. They only know deceit when they have been deceived. Then they only know truth in terms of its absence.

In this dreary situation, the Christian faith offers good news. Truth is not a concept. Truth is a person. Goodness is not a principle. Goodness is a person. In the midst of all the relativistic chaos of life in which people do not know what to do when the crises of life arise, Jesus Christ comes as a personal guide.

The purpose of this chapter has not been to explain how to convince postmodern people that universal absolutes exist. When we begin our philosophical arguments, their faces take on a blank stare and their eyes glaze over. Two thousand five hundred years of philosophical tradition is collapsing around us, but this has nothing to do with Jesus Christ. Jesus Christ is the only reliable basis for truth. Postmodern people have not rejected Christ because they have never known him. Once they know him, they will begin to learn the true meaning of the values of God from the one who said, "I am the way and the truth and the life" (John 14:6).

CHAPTER NINE

IMAGINE THERE'S NO HEAVEN: SPIRITUALITY

In 1977, George Lucas made a movie called *Star Wars,* which dramatically changed the theology of the average American. In that movie, a retired Jedi knight named Obi Wan Kenobi explains "The Force" to young Luke Skywalker, and anybody else who will listen. This Force that he talked about was a nonconscious spirit that permeated the universe, moved in and out of everything and held it all together. That understanding of spirit resembles the theology of Hinduism and Buddhism.

But the Force also had another dimension. There was a good side to it, and a bad side—the light side, and the dark side. Like the ancient religions of Zoroastrianism and Manichaeism the conflict in *Star Wars* was not between different concepts of the spirit, as though Christians would have a different concept of the spirit from Hindus; the real conflict in that movie was between the very few who believed there was some sort of spirit and the very many who believed that there was not.

Most of the people living in the United States grew up in the modern age, and the modern age is a world that denied spiritual reality—that denied there was anything "out there" at all. The modern world, so consumed with science and answers to every question, believed basically that everything has a material explanation, governed by laws that humans could discover. Natural science led the way with laws of physics, but we tried to find laws to explain every realm of human experience. Psychology has attempted to operate like a science to explain the human mind. Sigmund Freud applied this field to theology when he said that God is just an idea, just man's projection of his desire to have a father figure in the universe. Sociology and economics have sought to define their study of society and livelihood in terms that resembled scientific laws.

Karl Marx, the founder of Communist philosophy, explained human behavior, history, and destiny in terms of the great economic class struggle. The idea of God was just a ploy by the ruling class to keep the workers in subjugation. There's no God out there. There's no spirit world. There's just the here and the now, and then you die.

For the last few hundred years, Christians increasingly insisted "There is too a spirit world." There are things you can't imagine. There's more to people than the sum total of the chemicals in your body. There's more to the mind than just the brain. There's more to the emotions than just the nervous system. And we kept insisting that there is something. But unfortunately, something else happened over the last couple of hundred years with Christians in the Western world. Gradually we adapted ourselves to the modern view of the world and to modern methods. Liberals like Rudolf Bultmann and conservatives like C. I. Scofield both sought to establish a scientific approach to Bible study. If it were scientific, it would be better because science is the real proof. People like Charles Finney, the great evangelist, sought to establish the scientific laws of revival so that if we can just reproduce those laws, we will have revival.

In the twentieth century we have seen Christians who want to hold on to the church, the institution, the organization, the influence, but without the supernatural dimension of the Spirit. A growing number of people in the mainline church in the United States abandoned belief in an incarnation. They abandoned the idea of an atonement; they abandoned the idea of the Resurrection; they abandoned any idea of a real devil, or hell, or angels, or demons, and were left with only an idea of God. But a very vague idea. Certainly not a God who talks to us, who reveals himself, who sent us prophets and gave us his word. Certainly not that kind of a being. The God of dissipated faith in the modern era began to look more like the Force of *Star Wars* than anything else. Though conservatives held onto the old beliefs, many of us adopted "principles" of ministry that had been discovered scientifically. The Church Growth Movement provided a scientific way to accomplish our ends as though God were not even there. If you just use the method in the right way, something's going to happen. And we became functionally liberal.

Star Wars came out in 1977. That was the end of the baby bust. The baby busters were born from 1963 to 1977. Then we had what's called the echo-boom because the increased birthrate "echoed" the large birthrate of the baby boom. That echo-boom generation has grown up on television as latchkey kids with both parents working. They grew up in an officially secular country with a modern worldview that had no room for the spiritual. For the most part, they grew up without any exposure to church, unlike the baby boomers who were taken to church as children. This generation had virtually no connection with the spiritual and cultural tradition of the West. It was for them as though the past had never happened.

I think we sometimes flatter ourselves if we think postmodernity is an ideology opposed to Christianity. It's not Christian. It's quite un-Christian. But the postmodern people don't even know that the Christian faith exists. For the most part they have never heard the old, old story of Jesus and his love. For the most part, they have rejected modernity, which attempted to explain all of reality and all of human experience in terms of scientific laws. They have rejected modernity but not Christianity, because they have never experienced Christianity. At most, Christianity is nothing more than a vague rumor they have heard.

They know there is more to life than what meets the eye. There is something within them that is searching. They have a deep longing for something beyond the mundane of everyday existence. Nearly three thousand years ago, King Solomon said that God had placed eternity in our hearts (Eccles. 3:11), and three hundred years ago Pascal said that only God can fill the vacuum in the human heart. Baby boomers may be spiritually malnourished, but the echo-boom has been spiritually starved. There is a longing in the human spirit to have that void filled, and people are searching for it; but they do not know what it is, and they do not even know what they're looking for. These people are like the first-century pagans that Paul encountered all around the Roman Empire who had no sense of guilt because they had never known the law.

So we see a world now in the United States where morals are virtually nonexistent. The United States is like Jonah's Nineveh. God said to Jonah about the people of Nineveh, "Jonah, those people don't know their right hand from their left. But Jonah, I'm not going to blast them to smithereens. Oh no. I'm going to send you to tell them about me, because they don't know me" [Poe's Free-Flowing Translation]. So this new generation, the people that are now moving into influence, are like the Athenians on Mars Hill who experimented with a variety of religious approaches: a little Buddhism here, a little Native American religion there, a little witchcraft—because they are looking for something. Something deep inside them tells them there is a spiritual dimension to life. But they are ignorant of the Creator God who came into this world to take our sins away and give us life.

In this context of spiritual ignorance and experimentation, what opportunity do Christians have to reach the postmodern generation? First of all we need to recall that the Savior *is* exalted. He is over all. We cannot defend the Savior; he defends us. He is exalted over all other spiritual beings, whether they be demons or angels. That being the case, we have the opportunity to make known to this new generation the source of spiritual life. God as we can know him through Jesus Christ is not the nebulous, unconscious Force of *Star Wars* that we can tap into and take advantage of. God knows us, and he wants us to know him personally. The Spirit of God is not an impersonal force we can use but a personal being who desires relationship with us.

WHAT KIND OF GOD EXISTS?

The postmodern generation embodies American pragmatism. They look for a spirituality that works for them. Rather than condemn them for not having a lofty enough basis for their spirituality, we should realize that humans were designed in such a way that they would search for a spirituality that works for them, since the Creator is the only one who will finally satisfy. People often settle for something less. It matters a great deal what kind of God exists. Instead of trying to prove to the postmodern generation that God exists, we need only explain why the God of creation is the one who deserves our attention.

"In the beginning was the Word, and the Word was with God, and the Word was God. He was with God in the beginning" (John 1:1). The opening to John's Gospel is a famous passage of scripture, but it is a little bit confusing to our modern ears. What does he mean by "in the beginning was the Word"? People have explained to me since I was a child that John means that Jesus Christ the Lord, the Son of God, was in the beginning. Jesus was both with God and was God. Jesus Christ, the Son of God, who was with God in the beginning was the one who was the agent of creation. My Sunday school teachers had to teach me about this passage because we do not use this terminology today about "the Word" meaning the Son of God. We say the Son of God, we say Jesus, we say Christ, we say the Lord; but John was writing to people who did not know these terms because they did not know the Scriptures. They were not Jewish in their background. They did not know the prophecies. John wrote for a world that did not believe that God had created everything. The Greek world had a concept they called "the Word." The Word was a spiritual being that mediated between the physical world and the divine. By "the divine" they did not mean the God of Creation or the God of Abraham, Isaac, and Jacob. In Greek philosophical thought, "God" was both impersonal and unconscious.

The Hellenistic world had the idea of a spirit realm, a spiritual dimension, of which truth, wisdom, and perfection had a part. In ancient thought "the Word" represented this notion of divine truth, wisdom, and perfection that might be known. It was "out there" somewhere. People strove for it; but in the Hellenistic world in which John lived, in the world of Greek thought, people had a major dilemma. All the material world that was seen was considered evil or corrupt. It was the result of evil. It was the result of a demon, not of a creator God who made everything and made it good. All of nature and physical existence was seen as a terrible accident. Many people believed they had come from the divine, but that they had gotten separated from this pure spirit. As a result, people are stuck in their bodies. That is the reason for pain and suffering in the world. So the quest of life is to escape the body and remerge with this spiritual origin from which everything came. Striking parallels exist between this ancient Platonic philosophy, Buddhist thought, and current postmodern spiritual seekers.

John wrote for people of the Hellenistic world using terminology with which they were familiar. As he began with the Word, they would have said, "Oh, yes, the Word was in the beginning with God" and "Oh, yes, the Word was God." But then he began saying some things that were a bit strange: the Word was responsible for creation, and creation is good rather than bad. Then John explained the biblical view of creation.

Paul had done the same thing when he began to go into the Greek world. The Roman army had conquered the political world, but Greek philosophy and the Greek value system had conquered Roman culture. That often happens in great empires. The United States has been the preeminent world power for fifty years, and a great world power now for almost one hundred years. Yet, the United States is being conquered by a variety of value systems and philosophies. It is intriguing to watch as what has happened in countless empires in the past is happening in the United States today.

When John went to bring the good news of Jesus Christ to a Greek world, he had to turn their value system upside down. The new value system expressed in John's Gospel began with creation: the kind of universe that exists and where it comes from. John moved from the Greek worldview beginning with their idea of the Word. He said that the Word is not just a nebulous spiritual ideal, but a conscious being who spoke and caused everything to come into existence. A bold similarity exists between the beginning of the book of John and the beginning of the book of Genesis. John started at the starting place; he started at the beginning. In order to understand relationship with God, we really need to go back to that beginning, where we came from, how all reality in both the spiritual and the physical world came into being. We must deal with the goodness of creation. God made it good.

So if there is any problem with the world, it is not because of how God made it or the purpose for which God made it. The problem rests somewhere else.

WHO ARE WE AND WHAT ARE WE LOOKING FOR?

We live in a needy world. We live in a world in which broken relationships characterize discord that affects individuals, families, communities, countries, and international relations. We read in the newspapers about the way the neediness of people affects us at the local level: problems in schools, a family burned out of their home, a senseless murder. This neediness can be seen in the events in the former Yugoslavia. It can be seen in Somalia where people are starving, not because the country is incapable of producing food but because society has broken down to such a level of hostility one against the other that the crops cannot be planted and harvested because of war.

People experience need at a variety of levels from loneliness, to hopelessness, to low self-esteem. In the third chapter of John, Jesus met an unlikely needy person. This man was not like one of the beggars who came to Jesus, nor like one of the lepers, nor lame, nor blind, nor tax collectors or prostitutes. He was actually the most common of all needy people, somebody like us.

THE PURSUIT OF IMMORTALITY

A respectable man, a leader of the community, a member of the Sanhedrin, a keeper of the law, a good religious person, he was in pursuit of something. We are told that Nicodemus came to Jesus at night. He came to Jesus seeking something, but he did not ask a question. He made a statement, "Rabbi, we know you are a teacher who has come from God. For no one could perform the miraculous signs you are doing if God were not with him" (John 3:2).

Nicodemus called Jesus "Rabbi" and "teacher." By saying those words we know what he had on his mind. Here was a man who sat on the court of the Sanhedrin and was charged with administering the Law of Moses. The Law was the center of all that it meant to be a Jew in those days, and it was the center of whatever hope and expectation they had for immortality. Ultimately, immortality is always the human longing. Eternity is the human quest. We seek after something bigger and farther removed, some purpose, some goal, some completion, because we do not find it here.

Nicodemus had an openness to spiritual issues. Most people are religious.

Most people are spiritual. Atheism is not a major issue in the human race. Poll after poll taken in the United States lets us know that atheism is not a significant factor in the United States. Atheism represents a tiny perspective among the world's population. Most people believe there is something out there, and they want to be in touch with whatever it is. Paul acknowledged this when he went to Athens. He said, "I see that in every way you are very religious" (Acts 17:22). They were very religious people. The King James Version of the Bible says the people were "superstitious." Most people in the world are superstitious in their use of religion. That is, religion is the means to an end. Religion provides a way of getting something. Religion provides a way of making a deal. Religion provides a way of gaining power or immortality or something else.

That is the way that most people go about religion, and that was the criticism that Paul brought against the human race in the first chapter of Romans. He said that the problem with people is not that we are atheists. We have known about God from the beginning. The problem is what we do about God. We are not thankful to God. We do not give the glory to God, but we try to manipulate spiritual life and eternity to our purpose by the way we make religion in our own image. That is the problem (Rom. 1:20-23).

With Nicodemus we find a man who is open to spiritual issues but who is looking for something, because he came to Jesus. "We know you are a teacher," Nicodemus said; but his problem lay in his understanding of spiritual issues. With the court of the Sanhedrin salvation was a legal issue, which involved the keeping of the Law. If you keep the law, if you do it right, you earn the right to eternity. This would be parallel to Islam where the keeping of the law is the means by which people are perfected.

There are variations in different religions of the world about how to achieve perfection. In Buddhism there is "the way," the eight steps of the path; and if a person can complete this way of living, then he or she can enter into a state of *nirvana*. With Hinduism, people have a chance for living the right life. If a person can live right in this time, then in their next incarnation they can try to do it a little bit better. They work to be better and better in each new life; and if they finally get it right, then they enter into the ultimate state. If they get it wrong, however, they get booted back down to a lower form of life. If they get it wrong twice, they might wind up as a cockroach. This discussion is not meant as a joke. This process is very serious. This concept lies at the heart of Hindu understanding of eternity. The laws of *karma* govern one's destiny. So, even someone with all the outward advantages of life represents the needy, as does Nicodemus coming to Jesus. A religious person who has tried to keep the Law and do it right all of his life, Nicodemus sought out another teacher because something was missing.

THE PROBLEM OF HUMAN NATURE

As they begin to talk, something occurred that has always confused me about the third chapter of John. Nicodemus says, "Jesus, we know you are a great teacher come from God because of all your miracles." And Jesus replies, "You must be born again." It seems like a cog has slipped. The flow of words does not fit. What Jesus said does not go with what Nicodemus said. I often wondered if this bothered anybody besides me. I wondered if anyone else ever had trouble seeing the relationship between those two sentences, or if it was just me. Then I began to deal with the whole issue of what John is talking about in his Gospel. Jesus stopped Nicodemus dead in his tracks as if to say: "We are not going to talk about the Law, Nicodemus. We are not going to run down that path. We're going to deal with your real need. You must be born again."

The first chapter of John presents the contrast between the Hellenistic worldview of eternity and the view the gospel gives. The third chapter presents the contrast between the gospel and the Jewish worldview of eternity. This understanding of Nicodemus butts heads with Jesus. Jesus puts the issue right up front. He's saying, "This is not what you've always understood. You've got to rethink the way you look at the world and eternity." Jesus starts with the idea that people are the problem; creation is not the problem. Nature, or the material world, is not the problem. It is good. We are the problem, and the kingdom of God is not accessible to us. Try as you might, you cannot get there from here. Jesus is telling Nicodemus, "There is no teaching I can give you, Nicodemus, that will get you to heaven. There is no new trick. There is no method. There is no religious practice. There is nothing you can do. You cannot get into heaven unless you are born again."

This new line of thought threw Nicodemus for a loop. John captured the emotion of Nicodemus as he struggled: "I don't understand this. I don't understand what you are talking about, Jesus." Jesus explains that people are not by nature children of God. John started his Gospel with this idea in the introduction to the first chapter: "Yet to all who received him, to those who believed in his name, he gave the right to become children of God" (John 1:12). People are not naturally children of God. We are naturally creatures of the dust. We may become children of God, but the power to have that experience comes as a second act of creation by God. Becoming a child of God does not come through natural descent. Some thought, "Well, if you're born of the seed of Abraham, you've got it made." To them, Jesus said, "You're not children of Abraham. You are children of the devil." We can forget about inheriting a relationship to God from our family just because our family has always been faithful members of a church. It does not work that way. Nor do people become children of God through human decision, such as the exercise of spiritual disciplines, attitudes of thinking, or religious practices, all of which might just as easily be counted as superstition. Nor does it happen as the result of a man's will; such as what Abraham did when he wanted to ensure he would have a child when God was not on his timetable. Sarah had not conceived, so he went out and had a child by his wife's servant. We cannot rig our relationship with God. So, children of God are born not of natural descent, nor of human decision or of a man's will, but born of God. Jesus held a dogmatic and uncompromising position on this matter.

Then Jesus elaborated that the kingdom of God is for those born of the Spirit of God: "I tell you the truth, no one can enter the kingdom of God unless he is born of water and the Spirit. Flesh gives birth to flesh, but the Spirit gives birth to spirit" (John 3:5-6). The whole idea of flesh involves more than just being physical, though being physical is a part of it. In First Corinthians, Paul went back to the same idea. He said, "I declare to you, brothers, that flesh and blood cannot inherit the kingdom of God, nor does the perishable inherit the imperishable" (1 Cor. 15:50). The flesh and blood is going to wither away, but what is left when the flesh and blood withers away? This issue lies at the heart of the real problem with human nature. A change of nature must take place for a person to exist in heaven. Jesus said:

> I tell you the truth, we speak of what we know, and we testify to what we have seen, but still you people do not accept our testimony. I have spoken to you of earthly things and you do not believe; how then will you believe if I speak of heavenly things? No one has ever gone into heaven except the one who came from heaven—the Son of Man. (John 3:11-13)

Our little five-year-old daughter asks the big questions: Why can't I see God? That's a big question. The longer people linger around church, the more they train themselves not to ask that question and the more they view it as a child's question. Nonetheless, it remains one of the ultimate questions. That is what Jesus is talking about here. You cannot see God. That is the problem of the human race. We cannot see God. God is here. Why can't we see God?

HOLINESS AND SINFULNESS

Adam and Eve saw God. Why can't we see God anymore? Moses made one request of God. Moses wanted to see the glory of God (Exod. 33:17-23). It was not a big request. Many other people have wanted to see God. We often misrepresent how God answered Moses. The way we often talk about it, we represent God as saying, "If you look at me I'll kill you." That's not what God said. He said, "You cannot behold me and live." Those are two radically different ideas about why people cannot look at God. "If you look at me I'll kill you," is a threat. This view accuses God of threatening to punish people for looking at him. "You cannot behold me and live," is a warning to protect Moses. God withholds his glory from the human race because to behold the glory of God is to be destroyed.

Why? God is holy; we are sinful. Holiness and sinfulness cannot coexist. In that opening passage of John we read, "The light shines in the darkness, but the darkness overcometh it not" (John 1:5, KJV). Darkness cannot exist where there is light. My daughter Rebecca once asked me, "When Jesus comes back and when we see Jesus, will it hurt our eyes?" That question reflects remarkable insight. I do not think it will for those who are in Jesus. That's what Jesus tried to make Nicodemus understand.

People cannot endure right now the contrast between themselves and the glory of God. Isaiah experienced shock when he had his vision of God. He was in the Temple in the year that King Uzziah died, and he saw the Lord high and lifted up. It was a traumatic moment for Isaiah because Isaiah knew the scripture that if you behold God you die. He viewed it as a threat. He did not behold God; he had a vision of God. There is a big difference. God gave him a vision, and smoke filled the Temple. He was clouded. He was shielded, but nonetheless this was traumatic. He cried, "Woe is me! For I am lost; for I am a man of unclean lips, and I dwell in the midst of a people of unclean lips; for my eyes have seen the King, the LORD of hosts!" (Isa. 6:5 RSV). Here is a man who is scared nearly to death. Then an angel took a burning coal from the altar and pressed it against the lips of Isaiah, and his lips were cleansed. Now, remember, this is a vision. This is not physically happening. God is not torturing Isaiah. God is giving Isaiah an understanding of what God will do about what stands in the way of human experience with God.

At this point Isaiah was dealing with the same kind of issue as Nicodemus. He worried about how to have a relationship with God. Something was wrong, but he did not know what. With Isaiah, it was graphic. When he finally comes into the presence of God, he thinks, "Oh, goodness, now I know what it is. I am a prophet. My responsibility is to talk about God and my mouth is filthy. The holy things that I say are filthy." When you do your very best, it's filthy. That doesn't seem fair, does it? That is what Nicodemus was concerned with: the legal issues of being fair.

Zechariah had a vision of Joshua the high priest standing before the throne of God with Satan accusing him (Zech. 3:1-10). Joshua appears in his priestly garments, the ones described in the law of Moses. These beautiful, holy, pure garments are filthy rags. They are torn and stained, polluted and vile. The scene is almost comical because Satan stands pointing his finger and saying, "See! See! See! Destroy him quick." But, instead, the Lord has Zechariah covered with a new robe. This episode corresponds to the New Testament terminology, "robe of righteousness" that covers up and puts away that which is vile and offensive and a barrier. God does something about the problem. God changes the reality of the situation. This episode corresponds to what Jesus says to Nicodemus. The situation has to change. Our nature has to be changed. That transformation has to happen, because people are broken, needy, and cannot quite pull it off by themselves.

In the book of Malachi, Malachi describes this confrontation of coming into the presence of God and what it means. Malachi presents a scary image. Malachi says that God is "like a refiner's fire" (Mal. 3:2). Handel picked up on that phrase and incorporated it into *Messiah* as one of those wonderful and haunting parts of the oratorio. But what is a refiner's fire? If God is like a refiner's fire, what does that mean? When a gold miner digs a ton of ore, a certain part of that, but not much of it, would be gold. To get the gold out, all of the rock is broken up into little pieces and put in a pot, a big pot, a cauldron, and the heat is put to it. It gets hotter until, like a volcano, the rock becomes molten liquid. As it flows, the junk separates from the gold. The gold is removed and the junk is poured out. God is like a refiner's fire. All the junk is melted away so just the purity is retained. The problem for people rests in how much purity is present.

Psalm 90:5-6 speaks of people as grass that grows up in the morning, is cut down at midday, and withers in the sun until there is nothing left. The psalms also speak of people as mist that comes up in the morning; but when the sun comes out, the blazing sun, we are gone. Unless something happens to who we are, nothing will remain when we come into the presence of the Lord. We will be like morning mist. Because flesh and blood cannot inherit the Kingdom, you must be born from above. God must transform you.

In the background of all of this discussion lies the judgment, the final appearance before God at death. At the conclusion of the conversation with Nicodemus, John records these words:

"For God so loved the world that he gave his one and only Son, that whoever believes in him shall not perish but have eternal life. For God did not send his Son into the world to condemn the world, but to save the world through him. Whoever believes in him is not condemned, but whoever does not believe stands condemned already because he has not believed in the name of God's one and only Son. This is the verdict: Light has come into the world, but men loved darkness instead of light because their deeds were evil. Everyone who does evil hates the light, and will not come into the light for fear that his deeds will be exposed." (John 3:16-20)

The last judgment is not a trial. Americans tend to think of it as a trial. For at least one hundred fifty years we have dealt with it as a trial. In the story "The Devil and Daniel Webster" whether or not one goes to heaven is determined by a court case complete with evidence and arguments. Evidence is weighed; and if you were a little bit worse than you were good, you go to hell. That is a common American understanding of what the judgment is, though it does not represent a biblical understanding of it.

The judgment will not be a court case at the end of time, to hear evidence. In the American legal system justice is portrayed with a blindfold and a scale in which justice sees nothing and has no opinions, but in the Bible God sees everything. Nothing is hidden and there are no questions of whether something is "sort of" good or "sort of" bad. The last judgment is simply a matter of making the judgment.

In the beginning, God made a judgment. God saw the light that it was good. That was the first judgment. The last judgment will be a simple declaration: one is a goat, and another a sheep (Matt. 25:31-33). God knows the difference between a goat and a sheep. Sheep over here. Goats over there. God will declare the judgment, a declaration of the way things are. Jesus talked about this idea in the Sermon on the Mount. He said one's behavior is set by one's nature. Whether or not you can keep the Law is based on your nature. He said, "A bad tree cannot bear good fruit" (Matt. 7:18). It cannot do it.

When I was a little boy, my grandmother had a neighbor with an apple tree. My grandmother received a gift of apples from the next-door neighbor one day. She thanked her so very much at the front door. I went with her into the kitchen where she put them all into the trash can. She said, "They're no good. They're hard. They're wormy. They're pithy. It's bad fruit." The tree had not been taken care of; it could not produce good fruit.

HOW GOD CHANGES HUMAN NATURE

Jesus also said that one's nature is set by one's relationship to him (Matt. 7:21-23). He said in the judgment there will be people who say, "Oh, Lord, Lord, look at all the good things we did." And he will say, "I'm sorry. I never knew you. Depart from me." In him we are able to fulfill the will and purposes of our own creation. "I am the vine; you are the branches. If a man remains in me and I in him, he will bear much fruit; apart from me you can do nothing" (John 15:5).

That is the bad news about human nature. The good news is that Jesus Christ came into the world to change our nature and to make us children of God. God makes that change of nature happen when we trust him. The change of nature is quantitative. Eternity means the change of nature has an enormous dimension. Eternity is a long time. So it has to do with amount, but it also has to do with quality. It is abundant. Jesus said, "I have come that they may have life, and have it to the full" (John 10:10). God wants people to have real life, and to taste the sweetness in life. That kind of life happens because his Holy Spirit comes into us, abides with us, stays with us, and changes us. The apostle Paul explained it this way, "If anyone is in Christ, he is a new creation; the old has gone, the new has come!" (2 Cor. 5:17). Two thousand years later, he still offers the same change of nature to people living today that he offered to Nicodemus.

CONCLUSION

In the rationalistic period of modernity, Christians always had the danger of expressing their faith in precise, systematic form that often sounded like legal argument. Even while claiming salvation by grace, Christians could sound like legalists. The spirituality of the New Testament, however, is a relational matter and a highly personal matter. It actually fulfills the longing the postmodern person has for personal relationship as we saw in chapter 1. Rather than the impersonal spirituality of *Star Wars,* which leaves a person alone and without purpose, the gospel offers a spirituality based on personal relationship with God who gives purpose to life. The gospel story has within it the answer to a spiritual longing people are once again expressing.

POSTSCRIPT

Anyone who has gone to Sunday school for any period of time knows that certain subjects and topics come around like clockwork. We can count on a lesson about the birth of Jesus at Christmas regardless of the topic of the lessons around that time. We will always study the Resurrection at Easter. On a regular basis we look at the parables of Jesus and the story of the Exodus. Anyone using a planned curriculum will make it through the Bible every six years or so. This approach assures a general familiarity with the Bible, if not a depth of understanding.

During the spring, my Sunday school class studied the life of King David with attention to its contemporary application. I finished writing this book Saturday night, and Sunday morning we started a new series. We will not study a book of the Bible or a Bible character. For the next three months we will study the meaning of a biblical worldview. Worldview has never been a part of the Bible study cycle. Until ten years ago, very few people even discussed the subject. That a denominational press would break out of the lesson mold and address the subject, however, gives me great cause for hope.

In the past, only philosophers, sociologists, anthropologists, and missionaries talked about worldview. Scholars discussed it from the detached perspective of uninvolved observation. Missionaries, on the other hand, studied worldview because they were entering a world vastly different from the one they had left. It was necessary for them to understand the worldview of the culture into which they were going in order to communicate.

Like a fish unaware of the water in which it swims, most people are unaware of the worldview through which they make sense of life. They have never known any other way of thinking. We take a worldview for granted because it is always there. It is like the operating system of a computer. It lies hidden behind the day-to-day applications. Worldview represents "what everybody knows." Because it lies so deep rooted, we assume everyone else thinks the same way we do and understands the meaning of life and the universe from the same perspective we have.

Postmodernity represents a worldview in disarray. Postmodernity does not present a unified picture of the world. In a sense, it only offers a path of least resistance for a generation that did not have the benefit of nurture from its culture. A person acquires a worldview through personal acquaintance with people who hold the worldview. Postmodernity is not so much the collection of positive affirmations normally found in any worldview. Rather, postmodernity is the vacuum that occurs when no one is around to raise a child.

This book has explored various dimensions of postmodernity. A few pure postmodern people may exist in the wild, but it would be a mistake to think that all of these categories apply to everyone within a given age range or who live in a given geographical area. A person may have quite traditional views about universal truth, but have a nontraditional view by Western standards of what constitutes truth. They may be highly rationalistic in some areas of their life while being quite soppy in other areas. Even the person who does not want a fragmented life may successfully function as though only what can be known empirically can exist and at the same time hold deep spiritual views about the nonphysical world. In other words, many patterns exist for how postmodernity plays itself out. For that reason, Christians cannot come up with the perfect method or presentation of the gospel to fit all postmodern people. The effort to come up with the perfect canned approach to reach postmodern people with the gospel misses the point altogether.

Postmodern people need individual attention. Fortunately, Christ designed the church to give individual attention to people. Of course, you have to ignore the organizational structure of the denomination, the programmatic emphases of the local congregations, and the annual report of the church nominating committee for all of the committee and teaching responsibilities. All of this necessary clutter represents our "improvement" on the original design, but what Christ gave us is much simpler. We are a body of believers in whom he individually dwells bound together by his Spirit by which he makes us corporately one. In the course of life not covered by the organizational structure, program, and nominating committee report we have our opportunity to give individual attention to people.

Last Thursday night my family drove to Nashville to hear a very old man preach at the new Titans stadium. Two men helped Billy Graham make his way to the pulpit where he told about Jesus Christ. At the end of the service, a river of people emptied the stands and filled up the playing field. I had seen this same thing happen in Portland, Oregon, a decade ago and in Washington, D.C., almost a decade earlier. If you watch the people as they come forward, you will notice that few single individuals respond. In most cases two or three people come together. The most famous mass evangelist in history is not a mass evangelist at all. The secret to the Billy Graham meetings, which he has tried for fifty years to explain to anyone who will listen, is that they focus on individual Christians talking to the people they know. Non-Christians do not attend Graham Crusades, for the most part, because of the advertisements. They go because someone has invited them.

The Willow Creek Church in suburban Chicago adopted this same strategy to a church context when they first began. The Seeker Service is the big meeting, like the Graham Crusade. People do not go to the big meeting because of advertisements. Willow Creek does not advertise. Church members talk to their friends about Jesus Christ. Jesus Christ is the only good reason for ever going to church.

Christians need not fear the strangeness of the future. For two thousand years we have faced the strangeness of the future. We have survived the destruction of Jerusalem, the fall of the Roman Empire, the collapse of the feudal system, the religious wars of the Reformation, the industrial revolution, and two world wars. We have even survived the comfort and success of the establishment of the church as the religion of Rome, the schism of the Eastern and Western churches, the lustful carnage of the Crusades, the rage of the Inquisition, the sensuality of the Renaissance, the arrogance of the Enlightenment, and the hypocrisy of Colonialism. Our experience with postmodernity will largely depend on whether we view postmodern people as an enemy or an opportunity.

The loss of the historic place of privilege that Christianity enjoyed for fifteen hundred years is probably the most dramatic jolt of the postmodern shift. When I went to seminary twenty-five years ago, I first heard the common aphorism that Christianity is always just one generation away from extinction if we do not evangelize the next generation. That extinction has now almost occurred in Europe and draws near in the United States at a time when people are turning to Christ by the millions in regions of the world where Christ was once little known. The shift of status in the United States will help restore the apostolic quality of the church as people find no particular social, economic, or political advantage to belonging to a church. Postmodernity will help Christians focus again on the Person who brought them together in the first place. He has a great deal to offer postmodern people.

Christians lament the growing intolerance of the culture toward

Christianity. Though pluralism represents a major feature of the postmodern world, the exclusive demands of Christianity represents a threat to pluralism. It was so two thousand years ago in the Roman Empire. Rome tolerated a wide range of religions, but the Christians made exclusive claims about their religion. One difference between then and now resides in the place of Christianity within society in Rome. Christians had no privilege or status. Their founder had been executed as a criminal on a Roman cross. Their gatherings included slaves and women. Christians approached nonbelievers from a position of weakness rather than from one of power. In so doing, they conquered the Roman Empire through love.

We have a more difficult situation today. Whereas ancient Christians had nothing to fear but being thrown to the lions, burned at the stake, boiled in oil, or crucified, modern Christians have to suffer the indignity of not receiving the respect we feel we deserve. We can see our losses in historical perspective. The tendency is to think that we have a right to our place in society. Christianity has had a historic influence on the development of the West and the United States in particular. It is hard to let go of that place. We forget that we had that influence because society was made up, by and large, of people who owed some loyalty to Christ. We cannot retreat from the culture and be surprised that Christ is no longer acknowledged within that culture.

May Christians expect persecution at the hands of postmodern people? In many parts of the world evangelism is a capital offense. Governments execute people for sharing their faith in Christ. In those contexts, Jesus Christ represents a direct challenge to the entire social order. Unlike the hit or miss, nebulous vacuum of a worldview represented by postmodernity, the ancient and fully formed worldviews of the world, represented by Hinduism or Islam, and the more recent political worldviews, represented by Communism and fascism, cannot tolerate a challenge like Christ.

Postmodernity does not represent an organized worldview, culture, or mode of thought. It has no institutional form, like a religion or government. It is a moving target, constantly changing, and this book only discusses what it looks like in 2000. For this reason, Christians will not experience the same sort of persecution that Christians experience in other parts of the world. On the other hand, the vacuum quality of postmodernity will lead to forms of persecution. Whenever Christians are perceived as an obstacle to some economic, political, or social interest, people will lash out at them. The silversmiths lashed out at the Christians in Ephesus for hurting their trade. In the past Christians could speak collectively about immoral behavior and impose legal restraints on society. Having lost its special status in society, Christians can no longer impose their moral values on the majority.

Fortunately, we have been through all of this before. John Wesley grew up in this same vacuum. The issues were different, of course. The combination of deism, the Enlightenment, the morals of the Restoration, and the Newtonian revolution created the same kind of vacuum. Whenever it appears that all is lost, God does something. Awakenings have happened throughout history in which entire peoples return to faith in Christ. More often than not, the awakenings revolve around the young people. Awakenings seem to be a way God reaches an entire generation that the church has overlooked. It never takes many instruments for God to send an awakening. He seems to use ordinary people without much to commend them other than a willingness to take the time to help someone meet Christ.

The challenge for Christians will largely be one of attitude. If we want to save our culture, we will lose it. If we are willing to lose it for Christ's sake, we will gain it.

NOTES

1. I'LL GET BY WITH A LITTLE HELP FROM MY FRIENDS: RELATIONSHIP

1. Penny Marler and Kirk Hadaway, "Religious Marginality in America: Understanding 'Marginal Members,' " presented at an invitational conference for denominational executives, church practitioners, and social scientists, sponsored by Hartford Seminary's Center for Social and Religious Research with the support of the Lily Endowment, Inc., Orlando, Florida, October 16-19, 1993.

2. LIVE AND LET LIVE: PLURALISM

1. Fredericka Matthews-Greene, Address, Union University, Jackson, Tennessee, October 11, 1999.

2. See John Cobb, Jr., *Christ in a Pluralistic Age* (Philadelphia: Westminster Press, 1975).

3. See John Hick and Paul F. Knitter, eds., *The Myth of Christian Uniqueness: Toward a Pluralistic Theology of Religions* (Maryknoll, N.Y.: Orbis Books, 1987).

4. See John Hick, *The Myth of God Incarnate* (Philadelphia: Westminster, 1977).

5. Stan Mattson, President of the C. S. Lewis Foundation, tells this story of a man who is now passionate about his faith and who has had a long and distinguished career as a professor of English literature at major universities in the United States and Canada. On June 6, 2000, I had the pleasure of interviewing Dr. Paul Piehler by phone from his home in Canada.

3. GET YOUR ACT TOGETHER: WHOLENESS

1. Sir Arthur Conan Doyle, "The Sign of Four," *The Complete Sherlock Holmes*, vol. I (Garden City, N.Y.: Doubleday, 1930), 157.

2. Doyle, "A Study in Scarlet," 21.

3. See Harry L. Poe, *The Gospel and Its Meaning* (Grand Rapids: Zondervan, 1996), 223; Harry L. Poe and Jimmy H. Davis, *Science and Faith: An Evangelical Dialogue* (Nashville: Broadman & Holman, 2000).

4. TRUST NO ONE OVER THIRTY: AUTHORITY

1. The Editors, "Epitaph for the Eighties: The decade that was supposed to revive the nation's morality put televangelists on the 'dishonor roll' instead," *Christianity Today* 33:18 (December 15, 1989).

6. THERE'S MORE TO LIFE THAN MEETS THE EYE: EMPIRICISM

1. Stephen Hawking, foreword to *The Physics of "Star Trek,"* by Lawrence M. Krauss (New York: HarperCollins, 1995), xii.

2. For a helpful visual illustration of the train experiments, see the illustrations that accompany Stephen Hawking's article on Einstein in "A Brief History of Relativity," *Time* 154:27:80 (December 31, 1999).

7. CONSISTENCY IS THE HOBGOBLIN OF SMALL MINDS: RATIONALISM

1. Large portions of this section originally appeared as part of "What I Can Say," in *Youth Alive!* 10:3:22-27 (April, May, June 1991).

2. Edmund Grindal, *The Remains of Edmund Grindal* (Cambridge: The University Press, 1843), 379. Grindal's famous defense of preaching to Queen Elizabeth would be rephrased by the Puritans from Perkins to Baxter.

3. Theme from *Cheers* "Where Everybody Knows Your Name." Words and music by Gary Portnoy and Judy Hart Angelo, Columbia Pictures Publications. As Jennifer Harper states on her Web page about *Cheers*, "What I do know is that even in the darkest, saddest times of my life, *Cheers* was there. It transported me to a better, happier place, and for those 30 minutes the troubles I faced disappeared." See www.cheers.tvheaven.com

8. FEELING GOOD WAS GOOD ENOUGH FOR ME: TRUTH AND VALUES

1. Penny Long Marler, "Understanding Protestant Marginality," a paper presented at the Academy for Evangelism in Theological Education annual meeting at The Southern Baptist Theological Seminary in Louisville, Kentucky, October 7, 1994.

2. Anna Fynn, *Mister God, This Is Anna* (New York: Ballantine, 1974), 28.

INDEX